BOOK OF WOMXN

88

Spiritual Prayers, Decrees & Rituals

FOR THE DIVINE FEMININE

High Priestess St. Journey Is

First Edition
02/2026
ISBN: 979-8-234-01859-551999

Published by House of Melanite Empire
Atlanta, GA, United States
www.sumgoodjuju.com

INTRODUCTION

We have prayed in the name of Him for generations, to the Father, the Son, the Lord, but beneath the echo of those names, there has always been Her. She was the breath before the word, the darkness that cradled the first spark, the silence that carried the sound of creation itself. Before there were temples, there were wombs. Before there were altars, there were bodies. Before there was scripture, there was song, sung in rhythm with the tides, with blood, with birth, with becoming.

For centuries, Her name was murmured in secret, kept alive in the hands of midwives, in the rituals of women who remembered the moon, the soil, in the stories told quietly between mothers and daughters when the world slept.

This book is the return to the Divine Feminine in all her faces: the mother, the lover, the witch, the maiden, the queen, the wise one, the shadow, the light.

Book of Womxn is not meant to be read once and set aside.

It is a living text, a mirror, a spellbook. Each prayer is a key, each verse a doorway, and together they form a spiral, a journey through devotion, creation, power, loss, death, rebirth, and return.

Within these pages are prayers for the feminine soul. They were written for the womxn who longs to see feminine power in prayer. These were not meant to be prayers of submission; they are an embodiment of the feminine divine taking form again in us.

HOW TO USE THIS BOOK

This is not a book meant to be read in order, nor to be consumed in a single sitting. Book of Womxn is a living companion. It moves like the moon: waxing, waning, circling back to what has always been whole.
There is no wrong way to use this book. You may read it as scripture, as spell work, as meditation, or as poetry. You may open to a random page and let the words meet you where you are. You may read one prayer each day or dedicate a week to a single verse. You may speak them aloud, write them in your journal, or whisper them into water before you drink.

These prayers respond to presence. Read them beneath moonlight, at your altar, in your bath, or in the quiet moments before sleep. Anoint the pages with your tears, your oils, your laughter. Let them become part of your practice as language for your living.

You may also use the Magical Keys at the back of this book to guide your practice. They organize the prayers by intention, protection, love, abundance, release, healing, and remembrance, and offer ways to weave each verse into everyday ritual.
These keys are invitations: ways to translate prayer into embodiment.

WHY 88 PRAYERS?

88 THE INFINITE FEMININE PRINCIPLE

The Core Number: 8
In numerology, 8 represents power, balance, and infinity, the eternal loop between the material and spiritual realms.
Eighty-eight is a number of continuity.
In sacred mathematics, 8 is the number of infinity turned upright. It speaks of cycles that do not end, only transform: birth, death, rebirth; descent and ascent; forgetting and remembering.
When doubled as 88, the power is amplified. It becomes infinity mirrored. A sacred return multiplied.
88 represents the moment when the feminine no longer seeks permission to exist but remembers herself as eternal.
These prayers are arranged as a spiral, not a ladder. They do not move from "lower" to "higher," but circle through protection, abundance, embodiment, grief, pleasure, release, ancestry, mysticism, and return, again and again, each time deeper, wiser, more integrated.
This is the feminine way of prayer: cyclical, embodied, and fully alive.
88 is the number of "as above, so below," and is associated with:

- Manifestation and abundance
- Strength, structure, and endurance
- The continual flow of energy, creation, dissolution, and rebirth

In its purest form, 8 is the embodiment of divine harmony, the eternal dance between creation and destruction, expansion and contraction, birth and return.
These 88 prayers are meant to be returned to, revisited as the seasons of life change. What speaks to you now will sound different later. What once comforted may later activate. What once activated may later soften. In this way, the book becomes a living companion.
To pray through these pages is to step into dialogue with the Divine Feminine.

WORKING WITH THE SIGILS OF THE 88 PRAYERS

Each prayer in this book carries a vibrational pattern, a rhythm, a frequency. The sigils are the visual form of that current. They are not merely symbols; they are condensed prayers, mapped into shapes that the subconscious mind understands immediately. A sigil is essentially a doorway, a key. It is a living contract between intention and reality. When you work with a sigil, you are not summoning an outside force; you are awakening the feminine power already encoded within you.

What Each Sigil Represents
Every sigil included in this book is built from the prayer's core verse and its magical purpose.

WAYS TO USE THE SIGILS

Water Work
Place the sigil under a glass of water.
Let the water sit for at least one hour.
Drink it to internalize the verse's energy.

Candle Spells
Carve the sigil into a candle or place the sigil beneath it. Let the flame "carry" the prayer upward.

Write sigil on paper
Keep the sigil in:

- your bra
- your pocket
- your wallet
- a shoe (for road opening)
- under your pillow

They work beautifully in ordinary life:

- Set as your phone wallpaper
- Printed inside a journal
- Hidden on your desk at work
- Slipped under your mattress
- Placed inside a picture frame, behind a photo of yourself

Burning
Write or print the sigil on paper.
Burn it with herbs that match the intention (rose for love, basil for money, rosemary for cleansing).
Release the ash to wind or water.

Touch Activation
Trace the lines of the sigil with your finger. As you do, repeat the prayer's intention (protection, prosperity, love, healing, etc.).

Candle Activation
Place the sigil under or beside a candle of the appropriate color.
As the candle burns, the sigil "charges" and holds the prayer's essence.

FORTRESS

Book of Fortress is of divine defense, a litany of protection, a wall of sacred utterance. Here dwell psalms of refuge, decrees of safety, and prayers fashioned like armor. Speak them, and no weapon shall prosper.

Fortress

ENERGETIC IMPACT
WHAT EACH PRAYER ACTIVATES.

#1. The Throne Reclaimed — pg. 9 • Establishes a strong energetic shield around body, home, and spirit. • Deflects envy, malice, psychic intrusion, and ill intent. • Creates a sense of safety, grounding, and divine containment. • Strengthens boundaries without hardening the heart. • Invokes the protective presence of the Divine Feminine.
#2. Decree of Protection — pg. 11 • Seals energetic leaks and vulnerabilities • Wards doorways, thresholds, and personal space • Calms anxiety by restoring a sense of spiritual authority • Protects against emotional drain and manipulation • Reinforces sovereignty over one's energy and environment
#3. Road Shield — pg. 12 • Pray over cars, plane seats, travel bags, and doorways to guard against accidents, theft, and confusion on the road • Beautiful for commutes, long trips, and kids traveling.
• Before leaving the house, at the start of trips; Mondays, Wednesdays, and during Mercury retrograde.
#4. Reclaiming My Power— pg. 13 • Restores power taken through fear, trauma, or control • Protects against domination, intimidation, and energetic theft • Strengthens inner authority and self-trust • Reinforces personal boundaries and confidence • Returns agency to the speaker in all situations
#5. Evil Eye Remover — pg. 14• Dissolves envy, jealousy, and harmful attention • Clears psychic residue left by others' projections • Restores luck, vitality, and emotional equilibrium • Protects beauty, success, and personal joy from interference • Strengthens aura against future negative influence.
#6. Prayer for Justice / Psalm of Fiery Justice — pg. 15
•Call on righteous, balancing fire when facing courts, systems, bullies, or abusers. Can be worked for personal justice and collective/ancestral justice in community struggles. • Protects truth from distortion or lies
• Calls balance and fairness into disputes or conflict • Shields the innocent and restores moral order • Strengthens courage when facing injustice • Aligns outcomes with integrity and divine law.
#7. Curse Breaker – Prayer of Protection and Release — pg. 17 • Breaks active curses, long-standing spiritual entanglements, hexes, and energetic attacks • Dissolves ancestral and generational bindings • Clears lingering negative patterns or repeated misfortune • Restores spiritual autonomy and peace • Fortifies the soul against future interference • Beautifully paired with uncrossing baths, candle work, cord cutting, and ancestral offerings.

THE THRONE RECLAIMED

A VOW OF PROTECTION & BREAKING SOUL TIES

SIGIL

Suggested Use:

Speak it when you feel resistance rising as you step into something larger than your former self.
Use this prayer when:

- ***You are consciously ending an old season of your life.***
- ***You are breaking cycles of self-sabotage.***
- ***You are preparing to launch, lead, teach, publish, or step forward publicly.***
- ***You feel unseen, suppressed, or held back.***
- ***You sense ancestral patterns limiting your growth.***

PREFACE

Breaking a contract creates space. But acceptance is what fills it.
When old agreements dissolve, the soul does not remain empty. It recalibrates. It reclaims ground. It chooses again. This portion of the prayer is not about becoming something new, it is about consenting to what has always been present but previously restricted.
As you speak the words that follow, understand: you are not asking for power. You are agreeing to carry it. You are not requesting readiness. You are declaring it.

PRAYER

1. Great Goddess, Sacred Presence, wrap me in your cloak of fiery protection as I shed.
2. I now release and dissolve all vows, contracts, covenants, and agreements, spoken or unspoken, conscious or unconscious, ancestral or self-imposed, that bind me to suppression, invisibility, diminishment, lack, or fear of my own radiance.
3. Any oath made in pain.
Any loyalty formed in survival.
Any agreement born from abandonment, rejection, persecution, or shame, I revoke it now.
4. I rescind all permissions given to forces, systems, spirits, or expectations that are self-betrayal
5. I cancel timelines rooted in struggle as identity. I dissolve karmic loops that confuse suffering with purpose. I release inherited burdens that were never mine to carry.

6. All frequencies not aligned with my highest timeline, of freedom, service, prosperity, wholeness, and embodied power are nullified.
7. I call back my energy from every contract that drained, delayed, or distorted me. I call back my name from every mouth that misused it.
I call back my power from every place I abandoned myself.
8. What was signed in fear is now rewritten in wisdom.
What was bound in ignorance is now freed by awareness.
9. I now accept the full strength of my voice, my vision, and my presence.
I accept visibility without punishment.
I accept influence without apology.
I accept expansion without collapse.
10. I am here to architect divine systems of liberation.
I am here to build what heals what was once confined.
I am here in rightful command of my path.
11. This stands as proclamation, divine law enacted through my voice.
12. The way opens before me.
Support aligns around me.
Provision accompanies me.
13. I walk forward, fully in my power.
So it is.

❷ DECREE OF PROTECTION

SIGIL

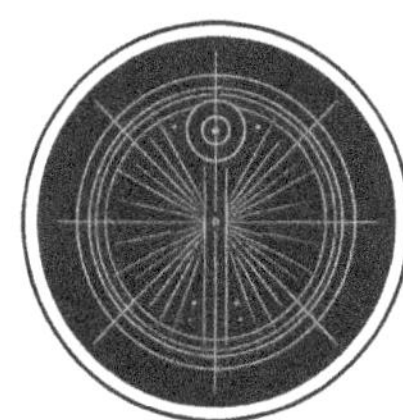

<u>*Suggested Use:*</u>

- ***When you feel spiritually exposed, unsafe, or energetically vulnerable.***
- ***Before entering new environments or unfamiliar spaces.***
- ***During times of fear, transition, or uncertainty.***
- ***As a daily invocation for grounding, clarity, and divine shielding.***
- ***Before sleep to protect your energy while resting.***
- ***When seeking the presence of the Divine Feminine for guidance and protection.***

PREFACE

This Decree is a sacred command of spiritual authority, designed to establish instant and impenetrable protection. It calls upon the power of divine light, angelic guardians, ancestral strength, and cosmic law to form a radiant boundary around the self. It affirms sovereignty over one's energy field, severs harmful cords, and ensures that no force misaligned with the highest good may enter. Spoken with conviction, it transforms fear into strength, vulnerability into empowerment, and uncertainty into unwavering safety.

DECREE

1. By the authority of my divine spirit and eternal will, I command a shield of pure, impenetrable light to form around me, now, instantly, without exception.
2. No energy, entity, or intention not aligned with my highest good may enter, influence, or attach.
3. All cords of manipulation, all hooks of projection, all spells of ill intent are hereby severed, dissolved, and returned to sender.
4. Angels of protection, ancestors of strength, spirits of sacred boundary, enforce this decree.
5. Stand guard at the gates of my energy field. Turn back all that seeks to harm, drain, or deceive.
6. I vibrate at a frequency that repels all darkness.
7. My peace is non-negotiable.
8. I am cloaked in the mantle of the divine.
9. I am wrapped in the armor of cosmic law.
10. This protection is active always,
while I sleep, while I work, while I dream.
11. I strengthen with every breath.

So it is.

❸ ROAD SHIELD

SIGIL

Suggested Use:

- ***Before driving, speak the prayer aloud or silently before turning on your car, especially when traveling alone, in bad weather, or on long journeys.***
- ***Keep a printed or written version in your glove compartment or dashboard as a daily invocation of calm and protection.***
- ***Pray it on behalf of your children, partner, or anyone you love before they travel, sending the blessing of safety with them.***
- ***Whisper or repeat key affirmations from the prayer (such as "Every mile is guarded" or "I drive in divine safety") to ease fear while driving.***

PREFACE

This prayer is offered to the Goddess as guardian of roads, thresholds, and movement. Whether for a daily commute, a long journey, or the uncertain roads of life itself, may these words be a spiritual seatbelt, binding you to peace, clarity, and sacred protection.
Call upon this blessing before you start your engine, when the sky grows dim, or when the road feels heavy with distraction. Let it be a ritual of grounding and grace.
Let her wind be at your back, her vision in your mirrors, and her love in every mile.

PRAYER

1. Guardian Goddesses of travel, I set out upon this road under the covering of your light.
2. You go before me to clear the way.
Guide my hands upon the wheel and guard the path ahead.
3. May your eyes watch the road where mine cannot. You ride beside me as my constant companion. You follow behind to shield me from all harm.
4. I drive in divine safety.
5. Let no haste overtake my calm.
6. Let no shadow cross my light.
7. Bless the wheels beneath me.
8. Angels of protection surround my vehicle.
Their wings a barrier against danger.
Their presence a shield of peace.
9. I arrive at my destination in joy and gratitude, whole, unharmed, and blessed.
10. For You have been my driver, my guard, and my guide.
So it is.

4 RECLAIMING MY POWER

PRAYER FOR PROTECTION FROM NARCISSISTS

SIGIL

Suggested Use:

- ***Before difficult conversations with manipulative or self-centered individuals.***
- ***During emotional distress or mental pressure caused by someone else's behavior.***
- ***At the end of the day to release lingering emotional residue and reclaim your peace.***
- ***At the start of your day to set strong spiritual and emotional boundaries.***
- ***When you feel drained, confused, or energetically compromised.***
- ***When you need to restore self-trust, clarity, and inner authority.***

PREFACE

In a world where relationships can become battlegrounds of the soul, where charm disguises manipulation and words twist into weapons, we must arm ourselves with divine discernment. Narcissistic energy, whether from individuals, systems, or our own shadows, does not merely wound the heart; it seeks to fracture the spirit's compass, making us doubt our own truth.

It does not curse the narcissist, but liberates you from their hooks, those invisible barbs of guilt, obligation, and distorted reality.

PRAYER

1. Spirit of luminance, clear my mind of confusion. Clear my heart of illusion.
2. Let me see with sacred eyes, and trust what I feel.
3. Protect my energy from manipulation.
4. Strengthen my boundaries without anger.
5. Let no charm or chaos distort my path.
6. I reclaim my self-governance.
7. I repel emotional vampires without absorbing their poison.
8. I restore my inner radar to recognize false light. I replace cycles of trauma-bonding with soul-nourishing connections.
9. Great Mother, You who see what hides behind the mask, guard my heart from the hollow mirror, from the one who speaks with honeyed tongue but leaves only hunger.
10. Grant me the wisdom to feel before I see,
the chill in the air when I enter their orbit,
the knot in my belly that whispers to leave,
the slow fading of my joy in their presence.
11. I call back my power, fully, calmly. Now.
So it is.

5 EVIL EYE REMOVER

SIGIL

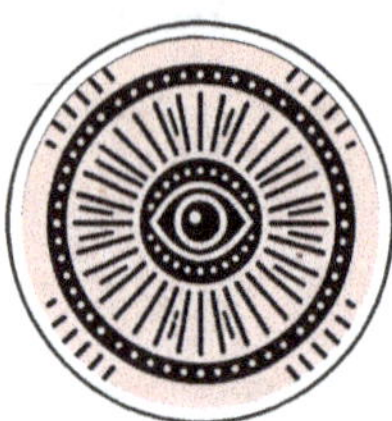

Suggested Use:

- *When you feel energetically drained or "off" after being around certain people or environments.*
- *After receiving intense attention, praise, or exposure (especially on social media or in public spaces).*
- *After conflict, gossip, or sensing envy from others.*
- *Weekly or monthly as part of a spiritual hygiene practice.*
- *Anoint your forehead, heart, and navel with a few drops of protective oil (like frankincense or myrrh).*

PREFACE

In many spiritual traditions, the evil eye represents more than superstition, it is a recognition of the subtle energies that can cling to us through envy, projection, or silent ill will. This prayer aims to remove the energetic imprint of the evil eye, whether intentional or unconscious, and restore spiritual clarity, self-trust, and emotional balance. This prayer supports women who wish to stay open and radiant without absorbing harmful projections or envy from others.

This prayer is designed to dissolve the energetic residue of jealousy, gossip, or unspoken resentment, and to wrap you in your own spiritual sovereignty.

PRAYER

1. Goddesses of Protection, I call upon your sacred presence to cleanse me now.
2. Remove from my body, my spirit, and my path, any gaze or energy that was sent with envy, malice, or hidden intention.
I release the weight of other people's thoughts.
3. I untangle myself from the webs of comparison, jealousy, and ill will.
4. I reclaim what is mine, whole and untainted,
5. Wash me clean of every trace of the evil eye, seen or unseen, spoken or unspoken, known or unknown.
6. Send it back to the source for healing, transformed into solace.
7. I ask my guides, my guardians, and my ancestors, to stand at every doorway of my being. Let their wisdom shield me, let their love restore me.
8. My joy is sacred and cannot be stolen.
I rise now, protected and clear.
9. No shadow may cling to my light.
10. No curse may linger in my name.
So it is.

6 PRAYER FOR JUSTICE

SIGIL

<u>Suggested Use:</u>

- ***During legal disputes or court cases / when facing false accusations or slander.***
- ***To dissolve the effects of injustice in personal or professional matters.***
- ***As part of protection work when dealing with harmful individuals or groups.***
- ***Before important meetings, hearings, or negotiations where fairness is needed.***
- ***Carry a piece of obsidian, black tourmaline, or tiger's eye when speaking this prayer to absorb and deflect negativity.***
- ***Write your justice request on paper, place it under the candle while reciting the psalm, and burn the paper afterward to release it to Spirit.***
- ***Repeat daily until the situation resolves in truth and fairness.***

PREFACE

This Prayer for Justice is a sacred declaration that calls upon the Divine and the elemental forces to bring truth to light, restore balance, and remove the influence of falsehoods and malicious intent. This prayer functions as both a spell and a decree, empowering the speaker to stand firm in their integrity while calling for the elimination of all that opposes truth and fairness.

PRAYER

1. The glow of honor washes over me and no shadow can hide from its gaze.
2. The voice of the Divine thunders in my favor, and every false word spoken against me is dissolved in the river of honor.
3. I stand in the circle of righteousness, where no deceit can pass and no injustice can dwell.
4. The path before me is made straight; the snares of the wicked are uncovered and removed.
5. Those who have plotted against the innocent shall be undone by the weight of their own intentions.
6. The scales are balanced by unseen hands, and every wrong is made right under Divine Law.
7. I call upon the winds to carry honor to every ear, the fire to burn away every falsehood,
the waters to cleanse every stain,
and the earth to hold me steady in my cause.
8. Justice is my birthright,
Truth is my dearest protection, and
Righteousness is my companion.
So it is.

PSALM OF FIERY JUSTICE

Oh Righteous Flame that burns in all things,stir now in our bones.
Make us living lightning rods for truth.
Our voices thunder, shaking foundations.
Where systems grind the weak to dust, where greed stains the temple of the earth, we plant our feet and declare, no more.
Let justice roll like sacred rivers, not the hollow gavel of men's laws,
but the cosmic scales trembling to their rightful balance.
We are the hands that tear down rotting scaffolds, the tongues that speak forgotten names, the dreams that outlive oppression.
Our very breath fans the embers of revolution.
By the power of ten thousand ancestors who resisted, by the unbroken chain of love that outlasts empires, we consecrate this fight, no rest until all are free.
Selah. Ashe. Amen.

7

CURSE BREAKER

PRAYER OF PROTECTION AND RELEASE

SIGIL

<u>Suggested Use:</u>

- ***When you feel spiritually blocked, drained, or stuck in negative cycles.***
- ***During periods of emotional heaviness, confusion, or persistent bad luck.***
- ***After experiencing manipulation, betrayal, or energetic interference.***
- ***When releasing generational, karmic, or unconscious patterns.***
- ***As part of a cleansing bath, cord-cutting, or uncrossing ritual.***
- ***When you are ready to reclaim clarity, strength, and spiritual freedom.***

PREFACE

This prayer is a declaration of spiritual sovereignty. It's a proclamation of protection, and divine authority. Its power moves to clear negative energy, dissolve psychic interference, and reinforce your energetic boundaries through the power of sacred language and divine invocation.

PRAYER

1. Mother of protection,
I stand with you now in the energy of authority.
2. I call upon the presence of the Highest Light to surround me, shield me, and restore me to the righteousness of my own soul's path.
3. I now dissolve and release all lower energies and spiritual forces that seek to confuse, control, or mislead.
4. I no longer agree to their influence. I no longer give them space within me.
5. By the power of divine might, I command all that is not of the Light to leave now, with peace, with finality, with no return.
6. I clear all energies of manipulation, deception, distortion, and oppression.
7. I release all patterns of mental fog, blocked will, doubt, and despair.
8. I unbind myself from energies of destruction, fear, obsession, and shame.

9. No thoughtform, no false voice, no energetic interference has power over me.
10. That which was sent with malice, I return to the void. That which was woven with envy, I now unravel with love. That which was intended to bind, I now use to strengthen my resolve.
11. I now clear the energy of rejection.
12. I remove confusion, paranoia, resentment, and unworthiness.
13. I free myself from bitterness, unforgiveness, anger, and the illusion of separation.
14. Pride, fear, and the need to hide dissolve in the presence of divine compassion.
15. I welcome healing where there was harm.
16. I welcome peace where there was turmoil.
17. I now invoke the guardians of light, the guides of my soul, and the Divine Source itself to seal this clearing with grace.
18. I am protected. I am whole. I am clear. I am free.
So it is.

EDEN

Book of Eden calls in prosperity, manifesting desires, blessing the work of your hands, multiplying resources, drawing the right people and opportunities, and living in a state of divine overflow.
Book of Eden is a garden of plenty, written for the prosperous womxn.
Here the verses call you back to the first paradise, a place of beauty, harmony, and divine provision.

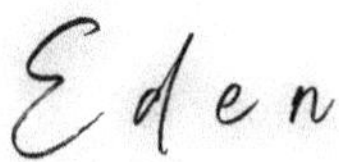

ENERGETIC IMPACT
WHAT EACH PRAYER ACTIVATES.

#8. The Code of Plenty — pg. 21 • Shifts your inner wealth thermostat • Ends scarcity thinking • Makes abundance your default state • Opens channels of income from unexpected places • Stabilizes long-term prosperity • Strengthens self-trust + receiving • Calls in luxury and overflow • Helps wealth stay, circulate, and multiply
#9. Prosperous womxn — pg. 23 • Draws patrons, benefactors, and supportive allies • Draws steady income • Opens doors to unexpected opportunities • Attracts generous clients/customers • Expands earning potential • Increases your "magnetic value" in people's eyes • Helps money stay instead of slipping away• Expands earning potential without burnout
#10. Manifestation Prayer: Command of Creation — pg. 24 • Amplifies your ability to speak reality into being • Strengthens manifestation speed + clarity • Aligns thought, emotion, and energy into a single creative-force • Activates your "creator identity" instead of "wishful thinking" • Solidifies your authority over your timeline and destiny
#11. The Entrepreneur's Prosperity Prayer — pg. 26
Boosts business visibility • Attracts aligned clients, not draining ones •Creates energetic protection • Tightens money boundaries, no more undercharging or pleasing • Repairs financial confidence, especially after setbacks • Brings mentors, guides, ancestors to support your work.
#12. Money, Power, Respect – pg. 27• Expands earning potential • Increases your magnetic authority in people's eyes • Strengthens your "leader energy" so others defer or respect you • Makes you harder to ignore, dismiss, or overlook • Strengthens negotiation power and professional respect
#13. Road Opening Psalm – pg. 28 • Dissolves fear-based hesitation • Calls in unexpected breakthroughs • Restores forward momentum quickly• Clears energetic and spiritual blockages • Removes hidden resistance or old stagnation• Creates new paths where none existed before • Aligns timing with divine order
#14. Luck & Divine Favor – pg. 29 • Increases your natural luck in daily life • Draws in helpful people and supportive circumstances • Makes outcomes tilt in your favor with less effort • Smooths away friction, conflict, and unnecessary struggle • Opens doors through charm and sweetness rather than force• Creates sudden blessings and happy coincidences • Encourages goodwill from others
#15. The Overflowing Cup – pg. 31 • Helps you stop settling for crumbs and start receiving in overflow instead of survival • Expands your capacity to receive abundance without guilt or contraction • Activates the energy of fullness, pleasure, luxury, and ease • Attracts generosity from others + improves financial and emotional support systems • Cultivates gratitude as a magnet for abundance
#16. Work and Provision — pg. 33 • Attracts stable, reliable provision (money, resources, support) • Draws in aligned work that honors your gifts instead of draining your spirit • Opens doors quickly where doors were previously blocked or stagnant • Pulls in unexpected financial help (bonuses, raises, side gigs, relief) • Reduces anxiety around survival needs

8 THE CODE OF PLENTY

A PRAYER OF ALIGNMENT, OVERFLOW, AND DIVINE ABUNDANCE

SIGIL

Suggested Use:

- ***You're starting your day and want to root yourself in prosperity.***
- ***You feel lack, comparison, or fear about money or resources.***
- ***You're preparing to make a financial investment, take a risk, or launch a creative project.***
- ***You're shifting out of survival mode and into receptive flow.***
- ***You're manifesting, vision-boarding, or calling in wealth from a place of alignment.***

PREFACE

The Code of Plenty is a remembering.

It is the soul's quiet knowing that lack is a lie, and that everything we need already exists within and around us.

This prayer is about aligning with the flow of life, trusting that what is for you will come, and knowing that you are already enough to receive it.

This prayer is a spiritual key.

It unlocks old doors where scarcity once lived.

It reprograms the inner voice that says, "There is not enough," and replaces it with, "I live in the current of abundance. I am open. I am worthy. I am ready."

PRAYER

1. I am born of abundance.
2. I am the living embodiment of plenty.
3. I am supported, provided for, and prospered in every way.
4. Abundance flows to me easily, generously, and constantly.
5. Everything I need is already on its way to me.
6. My spirit is aligned with the energy of overflow.
7. Opportunities arrive in divine timing.
8. Resources meet me exactly where I am.
9. I am worthy of wealth in all its forms:
love, health, peace, joy, and money.
I receive it without guilt.
I circulate it with gratitude.
I expand it with purpose.
10. I walk with a magnetism that draws in blessings.
11. I speak with power that unlocks doors.
12. I take aligned action with full faith, knowing the universe responds to my clarity.
13. My life is evidence of the Divine's generosity.

14. Every corner of my existence is touched by opulence.
15. My bank account, my relationships, my spirit,
all reflect the truth that I am already rich.
16. I bless my hands; everything I touch multiplies.
17. I bless my mind; my thoughts are charged with vision.
18. I bless my voice; it speaks affirmations that shape reality.
19. I live in a world that is generous to me.
20. I attract the right people, places, and possibilities.
21. I blossom without resistance.
22. I receive without apology.
23. I grow without limits.
24. This is the Code of Plenty, for it is not just written in the stars; it is written in me.

So it is.

9 THE PROSPEROUS WOMXN

PRAYER FOR FINANCIAL BLESSINGS

SIGIL

Suggested Use:

- *During financial uncertainty, transition, or goal-setting.*
- *Before engaging in money-related tasks (budgeting, bill-paying, investing).*
- *At the New Moon or Full Moon, when intention and release are especially powerful.*
- *Anytime you feel disconnected from worthiness, support, or trust in life's flow.*
- *Incorporate it into your beauty, health, or self-care routines to strengthen the connection between your sense of worthiness and your capacity to receive abundance.*
- *Speak the prayer to reaffirm trust, dissolve fear, and open yourself spiritually to solutions and blessings, even in uncertainty.*

PREFACE

Money is not separate from the spiritual path; it is part of the sacred flow of life. When we approach abundance with reverence, intention, and self-worth, we align with a deeper truth: we are not meant to struggle. This prayer is a spiritual offering, spoken from the heart of the divine feminine. It is for those who long to move beyond scarcity and into a relationship with money that is nourishing, empowering, and sacred.

PRAYER

1. Divine Mother, Spirit of Grace and Generosity, I open my heart to you.
2. I ask for your loving presence in my financial path.
3. Surround me with the energy of abundance, not only in coin or currency, but in opportunity, stability, and soul-aligned prosperity.
4. Divine Feminine Force, strip from me every vow of lack I swore in ignorance. May the flow of wealth reach me with ease and purpose.
5. Guide my hands to use what I receive with discernment and let me become a vessel through which blessings ripple outward.
6. I release fear and scarcity.
7. I embrace worthiness and divine provision.
8. As I receive, I remember: I am supported, I am deserving, I am enough.
9. May my home be warm. May my table be full. May my work bear fruit a hundredfold. May my rest be deep and unashamed.
10. With every choice, I walk in poise.
11. And so, with gratitude and trust, I receive. So it is.

MANIFEST

COMMAND OF CREATION

SIGIL

<u>*Suggested Use:*</u>

- ***In the morning to set the energy of your day.***
- ***Before important meetings, opportunities, or creative work.***
- ***When you feel blocked or stagnant and need to pull in fresh energy.***
- ***During ritual, spell work, or personal manifestation practices.***
- ***Stand tall, lift your chin, and speak the spell aloud with confidence. Envision the words wrapping around your desire and pulling it toward you.***
- ***The Universe responds to certainty, not begging. Speak this from a place of already having, not wishing.***

PREFACE

Within these words lies a fundamental truth recognized across spiritual traditions: that our internal reality shapes our external experience. What we hold in our hearts and minds, and ultimately give voice to, acts as a powerful force in sculpting the clay of our lives.

This "sacred decree" is an invitation, an invitation to move from passive hoping to active creating. It is a call to align your speech with your most profound beliefs, to use the divine gift of your voice not merely for communication, but for manifestation.

PRAYER

1. I hold within me the same eternal spirit of faith that moves through all of creation. It is the pulse of the universe and the breath of my own soul.

2.Deep in me, the old psalm plays: what I held as true, I dressed in sound.

3. Therefore, I choose my words with conscious intention, for I understand their sacred power. My voice is the instrument that shapes the formless into form. My declarations are the commands my reality must obey.

4. I believe in the boundless love and abundance that is my birthright.

5. I believe in the Goddess that resides within me. I believe in the perfect harmony that is always unfolding for my highest good.

6. And so, I speak.
I speak light into my shadows.
I speak healing into my wounds.
I speak peace into my chaos.
I speak gratitude into my present moment.
I speak love into my relationships.
I speak abundance into my endeavors.

7. I do not speak from a place of want, but from a place of absolute knowing.
8. My word is my decree.
9. The currents of creation move for me.
10. I call forth what is mine across all realms and all time.
From the deep and the heights, from shadow and from light,
through wind, through flame, through water, through stone, come now to me, for you have always been my own.
I weave your essence into the threads of my life. I bind you to my present, here and now.
11. I now vibrate at the frequency of my desire.
12. My thoughts, my actions, and my energy are in perfect harmony with its arrival. Free of delay, denial and detour.
13. Every obstacle is dissolved.
14. Every resource of good is summoned.
15. In the knowing that I am one with Goddess, I consciously choose my reality. My heart believes, and so my voice manifests. This is my law.
And so it is.

THE ENTREPRENEUR'S PROSPERITY PRAYER

INVOCATION FOR BUSINESS SUCCESS

SIGIL

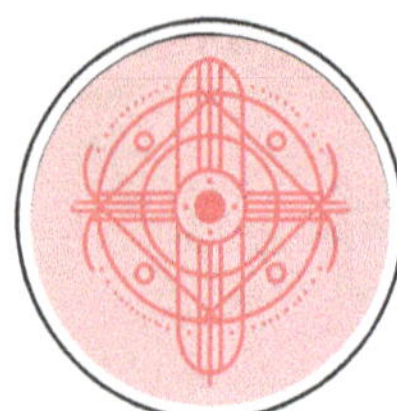

Suggested Use:

- ***Before launching a new project, service, or product.***
- ***Prior to business meetings, negotiations, or decision-making moments.***
- ***At the beginning of each month, quarter, or fiscal cycle.***
- ***During moments of uncertainty or when seeking a deeper connection to your mission.***
- ***Workspace Blessing: Print the invocation and place it near your computer, on your vision board, or in your journal. Let it serve as a daily reminder of your spiritual alignment.***
- ***Team Setting: If you lead a team, open meetings with this invocation or a portion of it to establish shared purpose and integrity.***

PREFACE

This invocation is a spiritual call to align your business with divine wisdom, ethical growth, and soul-driven service. It is not merely a request for financial gain; it is a declaration that your work is meaningful, your vision is valid, and that abundance flows best when it is rooted in perfection. It is easy to become caught in the metrics, profits, performance, and pressure. Yet behind every idea, product, and plan lies a deeper perfection: business is energy, and energy is sacred.

INVOCATION

1. I call upon the Divine Source,
Spirit of Wisdom, Abundance, and Right Action,
be present with me now as I step fully into the work I am called to do.
2. May supernatural guidance be my compass, discernment my ally, and purpose my foundation.
3. I invoke the flow of prosperity to move through this business as meaningful, sustainable growth rooted in integrity and vision.
4. Bless every decision I make.
5. May my mind be sharp, my timing divine, and my impact wide-reaching for the good of all.
6. May this business be more than a transaction; let it be a vessel of blessing, a channel for service, a sacred space where creativity meets need.
7. I open my hands to receive abundance,
and I open my heart to use it wisely.
8. By the light of divine intelligence and favor, I step forward. I build. I expand.
And so it is.

MONEY, POWER, RESPECT

SIGIL

__Suggested Use:__

- ***Speak this psalm aloud in the morning to set the tone for your day, calling in abundance, leadership energy, and respect in all interactions.***
- ***Recite it before business meetings, interviews, negotiations, or public appearances to step into your full commanding presence.***
- ***Use it as part of a money and influence altar ritual by lighting a gold or green candle, placing currency or coins before it, and reading the psalm three, seven, or nine times.***
- ***Memorize and speak it silently before entering spaces where you need to command attention and open doors.***

PREFACE

The Psalm for Money, Power, and Respect is crafted as a spiritual declaration for those stepping fully into their birthright of abundance, influence, and honor. This psalm is designed for women who walk with purpose, who understand that wealth is not only material but also spiritual and energetic, a force that attracts opportunities, alliances, and recognition.

PSALM

1.The gold of the earth rises to meet me.
2. The rivers of wealth find my name and pour into my hands.
3. Power crowns my head, and respect walks before me like a herald.
4. I am grounded in divine law, and so my steps are guided in abundance.
5. All that is mine runs to me with speed and certainty.
6. Kings and Queens recognize me, elders bless me, and strangers honor me.
7. My words carry weight, my presence commands attention, respect, and reverence.
8. Where I stand, the ground itself yields treasure.
9. Great Goddess has dressed me in the garments of prosperity.
10. I eat at the table of influence and drink from the cup of victory.
11. No enemy can block my ascension; no shadow can steal my crown.
12. I am wealth in motion. I am power made flesh. Respect finds me in every room.
So it is.

13 ROAD OPENING PSALM

SIGIL

Suggested Use:

- *During the New Moon to set intentions for fresh starts and open roads.*
- *Before important decisions or opportunities.*
- *After periods of confusion, delay, or closed doors.*
- *As part of spiritual baths, candle workings, or altar prayers dedicated to clearing and attraction.*
- *Anoint your feet with an oil (such as rosemary, hyssop, or frankincense) and declare, "Every step I take opens the way."*

PREFACE

There are moments in life when the path ahead feels blocked or uncertain. In these moments, we do not beg for direction; we align with it. Road opening is the sacred act of removing energetic and emotional debris so that opportunity, clarity, and forward movement may return. It is not about forcing what is not meant but allowing what is true to reveal itself.

This Road Opening Psalm is a devotional call to Spirit, inviting divine guidance to clear obstacles, awaken insight, and activate unseen help.

PSALM

1.Great Spirit, Cosmic Feminine force,
you who part the waters and break the chains,
I call to you now: make way before me.
2. Remove every obstacle, shatter every illusion of delay and rubble of indecision.
3. Where uncertainty once clouded my path,
I now move with crystal clarity.
4. Each step I take is supported and guided.
5. Every path of greatness before me unfolds with ease and purpose.
6. The unseen forces go before me, preparing the way in perfect order.
7. Every road I walk is made clear.
8. I meet the right people, the right moments, the right doors, all in divine timing, all with great ease.
9. No gate nor door shall remain locked
that is mine by sacred right.
10. May every detour lead to something greater.
11.With every road opened, I march forward now with open eyes and steady feet. What is for me comes under grace.
So it is.

⑭ LUCK & DIVINE FAVOR

SIGIL

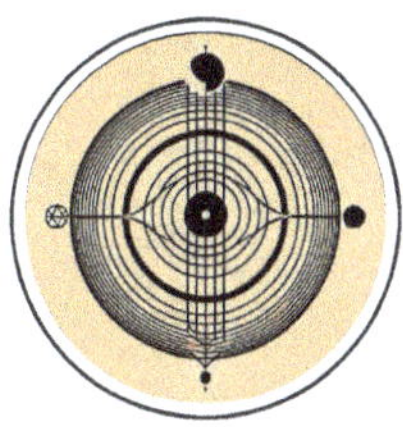

__Suggested Use:__

- ***To call forth divine favor, heightened synchronicities, and powerful luck in all areas of life, financial, romantic, professional, and personal.***
- ***Before business meetings, interviews, negotiations, or competitions.***
- ***Prior to making important financial decisions or investments.***
- ***When engaging in activities of chance or risk (lottery, contests, opportunities).***
- ***Speak facing east at sunrise to align with new opportunities.***
- ***Carry a small talisman (coin, charm, crystal) infused with the psalm's words.***
- ***Repeat three times before stepping into an important moment for an extra surge of magnetic energy.***

PREFACE

Luck, in the spiritualist tradition, is more than chance; it is the outward reflection of inward alignment. It is what happens when unseen forces move in harmony with our desires, our openness, and our readiness to receive. Whether you are calling in success, navigating uncertainty, or simply needing reassurance that you are not walking alone, this prayer is designed to attune your energy to receptivity, protection, and joyful synchronicity. It is a declaration that you are open to being met by miracles, guided by grace, and supported by something larger than luck alone.

PRAYER

1. I open my heart to the current of blessings that flows from the Source of all that is good.
2. May luck and good fortune cling to me.
3. Let favor be my dearest companion.
4. And so shall glorious opportunities find their way to my door.
5. Cover my path in protection.
Place the shield of light around my home, around those I hold dear.
6. May the gates of goodness remain open to me.
7. I invite favor to pour into every part of my life, in love, in work, in purpose, and in play.
8. Even when the odds feel uncertain,
Source, let your grace tip the scales in my favor.
9. I welcome success as my birthright.
10. May every detour still lead to my highest good.
11. Let good things find me with ease.
12. My life is the living proof of Divine favor.
My story is a testimony of unexpected blessings and perfect timing. So it is.

CONSORT PRAYER FOR LUCK

- **3 times → Quick, light activation when you need a fast boost of luck before stepping into a situation.**
- **7 times → Deep alignment with fortune energy; good for when you want steady, ongoing luck throughout the day.**
- **9 times → Full power call-in for major opportunities or breakthroughs—used when you're going after something big.**

Works especially well if you also touch a lucky token or charm as you say it, to anchor the vibration into something you carry with you.

WHISPER FORTUNE CHARM

Golden road before me, silver wind behind me, luck in my left hand,
fortune in my right.
What is mine comes swiftly; what I seek finds me now.
By light, by will, by divine favor,
It is done.

DAILY BLESSINGS WHISPER CHARM

I am a child of the Infinite, and the boundless favor of the cosmos is my birthright.
The wind of spirit blows prosperity to my doorstep.
The river of life carries opportunities to my feet.
The sun of grace shines upon my endeavors, causing them to flourish.
I am in the right place at the right time, always.
I recognize the right opportunities with clarity.
I am surrounded by the right people for my growth and joy.
I give thanks for the endless stream of blessings that flow to me, through me, and around me.
I am grateful for the seen and the unseen miracles that work on my behalf.
My life is not a game of chance, for it is a divine dance of favor and grace.
And so, I step forward into this day, lucky, blessed, and profoundly favored.

THE OVERFLOWING CUP

PSALM OF UNSTOPPABLE FORTUNE

SIGIL

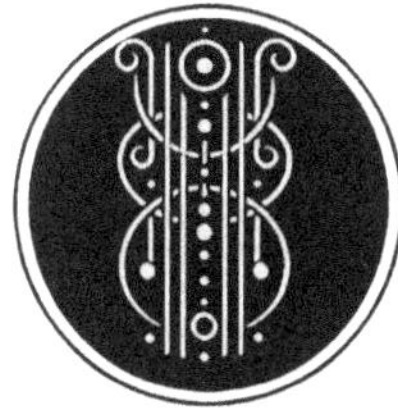

<u>*Suggested Use:*</u>

- ***Use it anytime fear, doubt, or lack-based thinking arises, reclaiming your truth as a vessel of unstoppable fortune.***
- ***Write down a line or phrase from the psalm and carry it in your wallet, purse, or journal to keep its vibration active throughout your day.***
- ***Recite it before business meetings, creative endeavors, financial decisions, or opportunities where you wish to attract favor and prosperity.***
- ***Speak it aloud at the start of your day to set a tone of abundance and unstoppable flow.***

PREFACE

The Psalm of Unstoppable Fortune is a high-vibration spiritualist declaration designed to align you with supernatural luck, divine timing, and irresistible opportunity. Its words act as a magnet, drawing blessings, chance encounters, and golden opportunities from both seen and unseen realms. This psalm is more than a request, it is an energetic claim of your right to walk in divine abundance and be in the flow of miraculous luck.

PSALM

1.The heavens open unto me and rivers of blessing pour into me.
2. The stars bend toward my path, aligning in my favor.
3. Every door, road, and window of blessing swings wide when I arrive.
4. Every gate unlocks at my touch.
5. The ground beneath me turns to gold and the winds carry whispers of opportunity.
6. What I touch prospers.
What I seek, I find and what I call comes running to me.
7. Lack is a lie I no longer entertain.
8. Scarcity is an illusion I shatter with confidence.
9. The currents of creation turn in my direction, bringing me treasures hidden and seen.
10. No misfortune can stand in my shadow.
11. No encumbrance can remain in my presence.
12. I walk in a mantle of favor, crowned in the light of divine fortune.

13. My life overflows with victories, my days are filled with miraculous encounters and abundance is my native ground.
14. Ancestors of enterprise, Angels of innovation, Spirits of sacred success, attend me. Weave fortunes into my footsteps, turn my labor into legacy, crown my efforts with exponential yield.
15. I am aligned with infinite supply.
The universe always says YES to my worth.
16. I am sustained by a boundless source. My well is deep and never runs dry.
So it is.

WORK AND PROVISION

PRAYER FOR EMPLOYMENT

SIGIL

Suggested Use:

- ***Before submitting applications or attending interviews.***
- ***In the morning to start the day with clear intention.***
- ***During times of career transition or uncertainty.***
- ***When feeling discouraged about your job search.***
- ***Write your job intention on a piece of paper and keep it on your altar or in your wallet as a daily reminder of what you are calling in.***

PREFACE

This prayer draws on the sacred principle that "Ask and it will be given; seek and you will find; knock and the door will be opened." By speaking it with conviction, you align your spirit, mind, and actions with the right opportunities, inviting work that supports both your material needs and your soul's purpose.

PRAYER

1.She who is Divine Source of all opportunities and provision, I come before You with faith and trust, knowing that You open every door meant for me.
2. You have said that when we ask, we will receive; when we seek, we will find; when we knock, the door will be opened.
3. I stand before You now, asking with a bold and open heart for the work that will sustain me, fulfill me, and allow me to serve in my highest purpose.
4. Guide my steps toward the right opportunities.
5. Let my skills, talents, and passions align with the work that You have prepared for me.
6. Place me where I will be of service, where I will grow, and where I will be treated with fairness and respect.
7. Remove any fear, doubt, or limitation within me, and replace it with confidence and trust in Your timing.

8. Open the doors that are mine to walk through and close the ones that are not meant for me.
9. I call forth the position that meets my needs,
supports my well-being, and contributes to my spiritual and material abundance.
10. I thank You for hearing my prayer, for guiding me, and for preparing the way ahead.
11. I receive my employment with gratitude, knowing it is already on its way.
12. From the four winds, I summon sustenance:
From the North, wisdom to steward my gifts;
From the South, passion to fuel my purpose;
From the East, new beginnings and opportunities;
From the West, the deep flow of resources that never runs dry.
So it is.

CONSORT JOB/OPPORTUNITY PRAYER

Repeat each couplet 3 times, letting your voice build confidence and flow.
Say it while walking to an interview, before sending applications, or during morning rituals.
You can also clap or tap your hands on your lap in rhythm to make it more embodied.

JOB-ATTRACTION CHANT

I am ready, I am clear, the work I seek is drawing near.
I am worthy, I am true doors are opening, pulling me through.
I am guided, I am sure, the perfect role is at my door.
I am grateful, I receive.
The job I want is mine with ease.

EMPRESS

FEMININE POWER

Book Empress is for the Goddess awakening, Becoming the ruler of her own soul.
The Book of Empress' is the key into the throne-room. These prayers are designed to ignite the divine feminine power within.
It is here to remind you of the power already yours. It's a magical manual of feminine sovereignty.

Empress

ENERGETIC IMPACT
WHAT EACH PRAYER ACTIVATES.

#17. Sovereignty – pg. 37 • Makes others respect your presence and your "no" • Increases self-authority + inner leadership • Enhances decision-making clarity • Strengthens personal boundaries • Helps you stop shrinking, apologizing, or asking for permission
#18. Sacred Courage — pg. 39 •Builds bravery for difficult conversations + life changes • Helps dissolve fear loops + anxiety spirals • Gives strength to leave harmful situations • Increases resilience and emotional stamina • Fuels bold leaps, new beginnings, and destiny shifts • Attracts opportunities that require courage but reward greatly
#19. Sun in My Steps — pg. 41 • Draws good fortune + daily blessings • Improves timing, alignment, and smooth pathways • Helps you "be in the right place at the right time" • Increases confidence, joy, and vitality • Repels misfortune, chaos, and energy drain • Illuminates next steps + removes confusion
#20. The Golden Feminine — pg. 43 • Amplifies feminine radiance + magnetism • Attracts admiration, generosity, and devotion • Enhances beauty, sensuality, and self-worth • Heals feminine wounds + internalized shame • Strengthens inner glow and outward charm • Pulls opportunities through allure, grace, and softness
#21. Glamour Magick — pg. 44 • Enhances personal magnetism + irresistible charm • Influences how others perceive, treat, and respond to you • Increases aesthetic glow, beauty, and presence • Creates a "celebrity aura" effect • Attracts favor, compliments, and social opportunities • Helps you bend social energy in your favor
#22. She Who Stands— pg. 46 • Strengthens inner backbone + spiritual endurance • Helps you hold boundaries even under pressure • Breaks patterns of self-abandonment • Anchors you in dignity, self-respect, and stability • Makes you emotionally unmoved by manipulation or judgment • Builds steadiness in storms + composure under fire
#23. Scripture of the Shadow Feminine — pg. 48 • Restores balance between softness + strength • Heals nervous system overwhelm • Increases emotional harmony, grounding, and flow • Stabilizes hormones + feminine energy patterns • Strengthens connection to intuition + creative cycles • Attracts relationships that honor your feminine core
#24. Beautiful Soul — pg. 50 • Increases self-love + positive self-regard • Softens harsh self-criticism and inner judgment • Draws friendships, lovers, and opportunities aligned with your true heart • Enhances emotional safety + inner tenderness • Helps you see your own worth + divine beauty • Attracts gentle people, kind experiences, and soul-nourishing environments
#25. Celebrating Womxnhood — pg. 51 •Strengthens feminine pride + confidence in your identity • Heals internalized misogyny + generational wounds • Attracts sisterhood, community, and mutual support • Awakens joy, playfulness, and self-celebration • Expands gratitude for your body and its unique journey • Creates a magnetic aura of fullness, ease, and feminine joy

SOVEREIGNTY

A PRAYER FOR RECLAIMING FEMININE POWER

SIGIL

__Suggested Use:__

- ***Speak aloud each morning or before important conversations to reclaim personal presence.***
- ***Use during the dark moon to release disempowering patterns and plant new intentions rooted in sovereignty.***
- ***Say this after shadow work, therapy, or energy clearing to anchor the power you've reclaimed.***
- ***Affirmation to Follow the Prayer***

"My presence is power. My boundaries are sacred. My truth is mine."

PREFACE

This prayer is a homecoming. Here, we remember that feminine power is not a singular note. It is the entire scale, the roar and the whisper, the stillness and the storm, the tenderness and the ferocity. It is the courage to be both gentle and unyielding, to lead with compassion and to protect with fire.

Speak these words when you need to remember your name. Recite them when the world tries to convince you otherwise.

Return to them as a compass, guiding you back to the truth of your own sovereignty.

You are not reclaiming something you lost.

You are awakening something that was always there.

PSALM

1. Great Mother, Source of All Creation, I call upon the ancient, unbroken lineage of feminine power.
2. I remember the queens, the witches, the healers, the poets, the silent weavers and the roaring revolutionaries whose strength flows like a subterranean river in my blood.
3. I am their descendant. I am their living prayer.
4. I cast out every false word I was fed:
that my strength is a threat,
that my silence is sweeter than my song,
that my flesh is a vessel for service alone,
that my soul must fold itself small to be loved.
5. I let go of the need to be palatable, passive, or perfect.
6. I unlearn the language of diminishment.
7. I reclaim my intuition as holy authority.
I reclaim my body as sacred territory.
I reclaim my voice as a vessel of healing.

I reclaim my cycles as maps to my magic.
I reclaim my rage as righteous fire.
I reclaim my softness as unassailable strength.
8. And I shall walk like a womxn who knows her worth cannot be measured.
9. I shall love like a womxn who cannot be owned.
10. I shall create like a womxn who births worlds.
11. I shall lead like a womxn who lifts others as she rises.
12. May my power be a healing force.
13. May my freedom inspire freedom in others.
14. May my wholeness remind all who witness it
that they too can come home to themselves.
So it is.

SACRED COURAGE

A PRAYER FOR LEAVING ABUSE

SIGIL

Suggested Use:

- *Speak this prayer when leaving a toxic relationship, habit, or identity behind.*
- *Create a Release Ritual: Write the name of your abuser or the word "fear" on a piece of paper. Read verse 2 over it, then safely burn it to ashes.*
- *If you are still in the environment or facing contact, silently repeat verse 7 like a mantra. Visualize a brilliant, impenetrable white light surrounding you.*
- *Use this prayer as a spiritual guide as you seek practical help. After reading it, take one small action: research a shelter, save a hotline number, or confide in one safe person.*

PREFACE

This prayer is a lifeline.
It is for the one who has endured the unendurable, whose spirit has been under siege, yet whose will to survive has not been extinguished.
Leaving abuse is not a single event, it is a sacred, terrifying, and courageous unraveling. It happens in the heart long before it happens in the home.
This prayer is for:

- The one packing a bag in secret.
- The one staring at the phone, gathering the courage to call for help.
- The one who has left but is haunted by fear, guilt, or doubt.
- The one healing in the aftermath, learning to trust again, starting with themselves.

PRAYER

1. Spirit of Strength,
I stand at the edge of my fear, my heart trembling but determined.
2. Grant me the clarity to see the path ahead,
and the courage to take the first step,
away from harm, toward my own liberation.
3. I choose freedom, even when my knees feel weak.
4. With sacred will and divine fire, I now sever every cord of control, every hook of manipulation, every chain of fear that bound me to this pain.
5. I am not owned. I am not captive. I am my own.
6. What was taken, my voice, my peace, my autonomy, I now reclaim my identity.
7. Make my steps quiet, my path unseen by those who mean harm.
8. Surround me with angels of fierce compassion, guardians who stand between me and all danger. Let their swords of light turn back every threat.

9. Their shields of grace absorb every curse sent my way.
10. I will grieve what I lost, but I will not worship it.
11. I am worthy of safety, kindness and deep love.
12. Lead me to those who will reflect my sacredness, the friend who listens, the advocate who fights, the healer who knows how to mend a soul.
13. Guide my feet toward a home that holds peace, a door that locks from the inside, a future where my breath comes easy and my body is no longer a battlefield.
14. My life begins now.
So it is.

THIS IS A COMPLIMENT, NOT A REPLACEMENT:

This prayer is a source of spiritual strength. Please combine it with practical safety planning. You are not alone. Contact professional resources for help.
Be Gentle with Yourself: Some days, you may only be able to hold one word in your heart, like "freedom" or "worthy."
That is enough. Healing is not linear.

REMEMBER

You are not leaving alone.
You are guided by the strength of ancestors who survived.
You are protected by a love greater than any violence.
You are carried by the part of you that never, ever gave up.
This prayer honors that sacred, unbroken part of you.
May it be a light on the path home to yourself.

SUN IN MY STEPS

SPIRITUALIST PSALM FOR LUCK & GOOD ENERGY

SIGIL

Suggested Use:

- *During new beginnings such as a new job, relationship, or life chapter.*
- *When seeking luck in love, financial improvement, or professional success.*
- *Whenever you feel roads are blocked and you need spiritual intervention. Hold in your mind the areas of your life where you seek blessing, love, work, relationships, or opportunity.*
- *Recite the psalm aloud with a steady and heartfelt voice. Best recited at sunrise.*

PREFACE

This psalm is not a request for material riches alone but for a deeper form of prosperity: love that endures, work that fulfills, and friendships that uplift the soul. It is a song of devotion that seeks harmony in all areas of life, trusting in the Goddess's power to guide, bless, and protect the seeker.
When spoken with sincerity, it becomes a spiritual magnet for luck, opportunity, and joy.

PRAYER

1.Dearest Spirit of Overflow,
I do not seek gold, I do not seek frivolous pleasure, nor treasures that fade with time.
2. I claim instead your blessing of feast and fortune, fortune in love that is steadfast and true, fortune in my vocation that is great and fruitful, fortune in every path I walk.
3. Open my roads to bountiful opportunity.
4. Guide my steps to jubilance.
5. Crown my days with serenity
and surround me with friendships that uplift, connections that inspire growth, laughter, and courage.
6. Let good energy rise like morning sun in my bones: a golden thread from root to crown,
a hummingbird in my chest, a quiet knowing that all is well.
7. I declare happiness that does not waver, prosperity that nourishes, and love that endures.

8. O Spirit of Plenty, Goddess of Abundance,
let your light guide me and your favor rest upon me.
9. Let my life be rich in moments. I invite the light that does not burn but warms. I invite the laughter that springs from no reason. I invite the small miracles: a stranger's kindness, a sip of cool water,
the unexpected bloom in dry ground.
10. The wind of high fortune fills my sails. It carries me gently toward harmonious encounters, prosperous outcomes, and happy coincidences. I am carried by a grace greater than my own striving.
11. I welcome abundance in all forms
knowing as I receive, so too shall I give.
So it is.

COMPANION LUCK PRAYER

DECREE OF MIRACULOUS MAGNETISM

My energy is a magnet for miracles.
Every thought I think, every word I speak, and every action I take is charged with the frequency of miraculous manifestation.
I am a living invitation to grace, synchronicity, and wonder.
My very presence calls in blessings, breakthroughs, and divine surprises.
The universe conspires in my favor.

THE GOLDEN FEMININE

FEMININE SPIRITUALIST CONFIDENCE DECREE

SIGIL

Suggested Use:

- *Each morning to set the tone for your day.*
- *Before important events, performances, or speaking engagements.*
- *During moments of self-doubt or emotional challenge.*
- *Anytime you want to strengthen your energy and presence.*
- *Pair the decree with power poses or gentle swaying movements to embody the energy physically as well as spiritually.*

PREFACE

This prayer-decree declares what already is. Speaking it is an act of spiritual alignment, calling forth the version of you who knows her worth and lives it fully. With each repetition, you reinforce your energetic field, dismantle doubt, and fortify your confidence in both the seen and unseen realms. It is a spoken embodiment of self-assurance, divine power, and unapologetic presence. Rooted in spiritualist principles, it affirms that confidence is not something to chase; it is a birthright woven into your very being by the Creator.

DECREE

1. By the power of divine rightness, I declare:
I am a walking miracle, crafted by cosmic hands, animated by sacred breath.
2. Every cell of my being vibrates with inherent worth.
3. My presence commands spaces, free of force but by the magnetic authority of my authenticity.
4. Where I stand is holy ground.
5. Doubt has no home here.
6. I evict every whisper of inadequacy; my mind is a fortress of divinity.
7. I speak in boldness, my voice an instrument of liberation. My words carry weight because they flow into new universes.
8. Failure bows before me, as fuel for my evolution.
9. Every "no" is divine redirection.
10. I refuse to recede. The world needs my full expression.
11. I occupy my destiny without apology.
What others call "confidence" is simply my remembrance: I am Goddess in motion.
So it is.

21

GLAMOUR MAGICK

SIGIL

Suggested Use:
- ***Embody your inner enchantress before a special event or public appearance.***
- ***Ground yourself in self-worth before a date, meeting, or creative performance.***
- ***Begin the day in beauty and intention, aligning energy before dressing or adorning.***
- ***Reconnect to your power when self-doubt or insecurity arises.***
- ***Repeat it while getting dressed or applying oils/makeup.***
- ***Speak the prayer aloud slowly, gazing into your own eyes.***
- ***Breathe deeply between verses. Feel the words settle into your body.***

PREFACE

Glamour is revelation. It is the sacred practice of dressing in your own energy, shaping your aura with intention, and letting your essence shimmer through your presence.
It is a form of communion with the unseen. This is not about changing yourself to be accepted; it is about amplifying what is already divine. This is glamour as energy, as embodiment, as self-love made luminous.
Let this prayer be your reflection.
Let it be your affirmation.
Let it be your permission to shine.

PRAYER

1. Spirit of Delight, I awaken now to the enchantment of my own being.
2. I see myself as beautiful, deeply, truly, holy. And so does the world around me, for it recognizes the glow of one who remembers herself.
3. My voice carries the cadence of dance and confidence.
4. Every word I speak ripples with calm command.
5. When I speak, the world listens.
6. I move with sweet intention.
7. I dress with devotion.
8. I adorn myself in celebration of who I am, fully embodied in this heavenly vessel.
9. My aura is magnetic.
10. Let my inner sun rise to meet the day, that my outer form may shine with its truth.
11. I parade in magnificence, and beauty follows me.
12. I decree that all who look upon me see the aura of majesty I choose to project. My stride weaves spells. My gaze holds galaxies.

13. May my glamour manipulate none, but inspire all.
May it obscure nothing, but reveal the light of my spirit.
14. Let my beauty be a door, an invitation for others to remember their own light.
15. I awaken the ancient art of glamour within me.
16. I magnify the brilliance already alive within me.
17. Let my magnetism draw only what serves my highest good,
wanted attention, respectful admiration, aligned opportunities.
18. Let confusion, envy, and ill intent slide from my energy field
like water from a stone.
19. The world feels my glow.
20. The world welcomes my light
because I choose to shine without restraint.
So it is.

SHE WHO STANDS

FEMININE DECREE FOR PERSONAL POWER

SIGIL

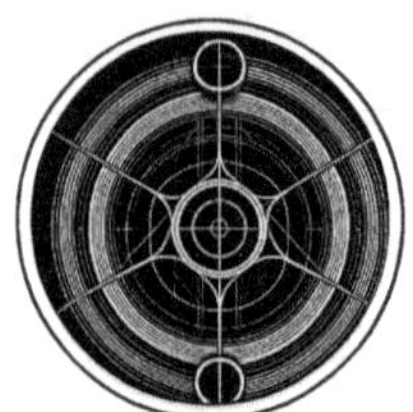

Suggested Use:

- *Upon waking to set a tone of strength for the day.*
- *During challenges or spiritual battles.*
- *Before stepping into leadership, creative work, or decision-making.*
- *When you feel drained, disempowered, or disconnected from your inner fire.*
- *To dissolve feelings of powerlessness, awaken divine courage, and anchor your identity in victory and abundance.*
- *Speak the decree aloud with steady conviction, allowing each line to resonate fully in your body and spirit.*

PREFACE

This decree calls in the abundant life force of the Divine, the courage to stand boldly in your truth, and the joy that fuels perseverance even in seasons of darkness. It reminds you that your "winning season" is not determined by external conditions but by the spiritual alignment of your heart, mind, and soul.
Spoken with conviction, this decree shifts your energy from doubt to certainty, from fear to faith, and from passivity to active creation. It embodies the spiritualist truth that your light, once claimed, becomes an unstoppable force in shaping your destiny.

DECREE

1. I profess my rightful place in the flow of life.
2. The power within me is ancient and divinely sourced.
3. I am seen, I am heard, and I am felt.
4. No person, no circumstance, and no past moment holds dominion over me.
5. I release every chain, visible and invisible, that has sought to bind me.
6. I am the unbroken axis of my own existence, wisdom carved in bone, strength like tectonic force, my will a beacon that bends reality to its doing.
7. I am filled with life abundantly; my presence is potent. My focus is unwavering.
8. By the unbreakable will of the Divine Feminine within me, I claim mastery over my mind, my body, and my spirit.
9. I am the sole authority of my being.
Life's power ascends within me, flowing from the crown of my head to the soles of my feet.
10. Let doubters choke on their disbelief of my power; my essence shall never be up for debate.

11. I take ownership of my spirit, my attention, my focus, my vitality.
12. I call back all energy lost to doubt, distraction, or people-pleasing.
13. My choices shape my reality.
14. My energy transforms everything it touches for my highest good.
15. Even in the darkness, I am in my winning season.

I rise undefeated, collecting victory in every step, for my path is blessed and my outcome is assured.

So it is.

SCRIPTURE OF THE SHADOW FEMININE

SIGIL

Suggested Use:

- ***Use it to call forth the hidden aspects of the self with reverence and courage.***
- ***After reading the scripture, ask yourself:
  What part of my shadow wants to be seen today?
  Where have I mistaken wildness for wrongness?***
- ***Use the scripture to invoke the energy of Kali, Lilith, Hecate, or other dark goddess archetypes.***
- ***Read verses aloud at the beginning of a shadow work session or journaling ritual.***

PREFACE

This scripture is not for the faint-hearted. It is for the ones who remember in their bones what the world told them to forget.
It is for the women who swallowed their fire to survive. The Shadow Feminine is not your enemy. They feared her because she could not be ruled.
This scripture will lead you back into your sacred center. Back to the throne you were taught to abandon.
A resurrection of the Shadow Feminine is not to be subdued, she's meant to be witnessed, welcomed, and worshiped.

PSALM

1. I call forth the exiled parts of my soul. To the one who learned to hide her rage, her sorrow, her primal power: you are welcome here.
2. I break the vows that trained me to be the pause in the music, never the note, nor the song.
3. Let the wild one within, the untamed and knowing one, step forward. Rage is not her sickness. Rage is her first honest breath after a century of silence.
4. Dearest shadow, no longer shall I banish you into docility. I will build a hearth for you in the center of my heart. Bring your hidden gifts into the light of my consciousness.
5. And those who feared her shall kneel in awe. For she is the unveiling.
6. She devours illusion. She midwives revelation.
7. Honor her in your chaos. Sing her name in your shame. She is the sacred dark that makes the dawn holy.
8. Blessed are the women who dare dance in her name. Blessed is the womxn who makes peace with her own darkness. So it is.

COMPANION SCRIPTURE OF THE SHADOW FEMININE PRAYER

FEMININE ESSENCE & BALANCE

Source of All Nurturing Life,
You who dance in the curve of the moon and the turn
of the tide, awaken in me the deep, knowing essence of the
Sacred Feminine, as a way of being.
I honor the softness that soothes and the fierceness
that protects.
I embrace the stillness that listens and the voice that
sings new paradigms into view.
I welcome the patience that endures and the passion
that creates. In this balance, I find my wholeness.
Great Spirit, teach me to receive as sacred allowing, not the passivity of
surrender.
Like the earth drinking rain, like the night holding stars, like the womb
nurturing life.
I am a vessel of divine grace.
I unite the warrior and the healer within me.
I marry intuition and action.
I weave together body and spirit.
No part of me is out of place.
No aspect of me is without purpose.
I honor the divine feminine within me, she who speaks through color, sound,
tone and texture, creates through love and listens with her whole being.
Divine Mother, surround me in your warmth, root me in your strength.
May I become the bridge where creation and direction walk as one.
May my presence bring comfort and courage.
May my life be a prayer of balance, a testament to the power of gentleness,
the power within vulnerability, the wisdom in cycles
and the divinity of being fully womxn.
So it is.

BEAUTIFUL SOUL

PRAYER OF BEAUTY AND INNER RADIANCE

SIGIL

<u>Suggested Use:</u>

- ***Read when struggling with self-image, comparison, or depletion. When you want to soften but also need structure.***
- ***Restores inner harmony, helping you see yourself as sacred creation rather than project or performance. When you desire to be both receptive and empowered.***
- ***Use before photoshoots, performances, or social events to activate authentic magnetism.***
- ***Activates the Heart and Solar Plexus Chakras, awakening warmth, confidence, and luminous self-appreciation.***

PREFACE

In a world that teaches us to look outward for validation, this prayer is an invitation to return inward, to the place where beauty begins: within the spirit. It is a spiritual practice of re-seeing ourselves, of calling our attention back to what is already glowing beneath the surface. It is about reclaiming authorship over how we feel about ourselves and recognizing that adornment, style, and glamour can be joyful tools, but they are not the root of our worth. May these words remind you of what you already are: magnetic.

You are not waiting to become beautiful. You already are.

And now, you begin to speak that truth.

PRAYER

1. Cosmic Feminine Force, set me free from narrow visions of beauty.
2. I release the need to compare, to perform, to chase approval. I let go of every invalid story that told me I was not enough. I dissolve every standard that made me question my worth.
3. I anoint my spirit with oils of gladness and peace.
4. I praise the shape, color, texture, and rhythm of my being. I know I am worthy, dressed or bare, quiet or bold.
5. I adorn myself with jewels of sweetness made bright and wrap my being in garments of merciful light.
6. The beauty I seek, I already am.
A unique and brilliant note in the great I AM.
I carry the dawn-star within my own soul;
perfect, beloved, and radiantly whole.
7. When I look upon my own face, let me recognize the Divine staring back.
I am beauty in motion.
So it is.

25 CELEBRATING WOMXNHOOD

SIGIL

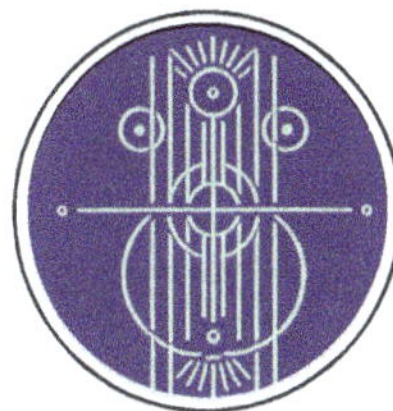

Suggested Use:

- *To open a gathering of women (a circle, a meeting, a simple get-together), have one person read it aloud or go around and have each womxn read a verse.*
- *Place items on your altar that represent different aspects of your womxnhood (a photo, a stone, a piece of jewelry, a written intention). Read the psalm as a way to consecrate the space and these symbols of your journey.*
- *Write the psalm out on beautiful stationery and give it to a sister, friend, or mentor as a blessing. Tell her which verse made you think of her.*
- *On your birthday, menstrual cycle milestone, or any personal anniversary, light a candle in your favorite color. Read the psalm aloud to yourself.*

PREFACE

This psalm is an offering, a sacred pause in the whirl of life to honor the profound, often unsung, miracle of being a womxn.

It is written for the girl stepping into her power, for the mother nurturing life in all its forms, for the warrior healing generational wounds, and for the elder whose presence is a living library of wisdom. It is for those who identify with the creative, resilient, and intuitive spirit of the feminine journey.

Here, we do not celebrate a single ideal. We honor the full spectrum, the soft and the fierce, the quiet and the loud, the gentle and the unyielding. This is a tribute to the divinity found in everyday acts of love, courage, and presence.

PRAYER

1. All praise due to womxn, the keepers of life.
2. We are the weavers of story, the singers of soul, the bringers of light to the breaking of dawn.
3. We honor the bodies that have borne life and laughter, scarred and soft, powerful and patient, temples of experience, maps of memory, each curve a testament, each line a legacy.
4. Blessed is the womxn who knows her own mind, who speaks her truth, who nurtures and negotiates, creates and commands, who leads not over others, but beside them.
5. We celebrate the sisters who stand together, the circle of strength that raises each voice, the shared glance of knowing, the hands that hold fast, the love that says: You are not alone.
6. Let us rejoice in the girl not yet grown, the elder whose eyes hold a thousand sunsets, and every womxn awakening somewhere between, for each season sacred.
7. For we are life's poets and prophets and pioneers, and the world is richer for every womxn in it. So be it.

Book of Qadshu carries the energy of love, beauty, and sacred pleasure. Qadshu teaches that sex is not shame, its nourishment, joy that opens the heart and multiplies life. Book of Qadshu verses bless intimacy, awaken desire as divine power, and crown the body as a temple of delight.

It naturally centers on spells where pleasure, beauty, and love are gateways to power

QADSHU

(KAH-DESH)

SENSUALITY

Qadshu

ENERGETIC IMPACT
WHAT EACH PRAYER ACTIVATES.

#26. Pussy Prayer — pg. 54 • Awakens sacred sensual energy and erotic confidence • Strengthens boundaries and increases discernment in intimacy • Heals shame, repression, and fear around sexuality • Deepens embodiment and pleasure without apology • Inspires self-trust, self-devotion, and sensual authority • Helps you choose lovers, partners, and experiences from clarity, not from wounds.

#27. Sensual Soul — pg. 56 • Reawakens passion after numbness, heartbreak, or stress • Amplifies allure, charm, romantic presence, and sexual receptivity • Enhances connection between pleasure, intuition, and creativity • Opens the heart-womb channel, deepening emotional + erotic bonding • Encourages slow living, savoring, embodiment, and sensual ritual • Attracts lovers, partners, and admirers who honor your sensual nature

#28.The Gospel of Pleasure — pg. 58 • Activates seduction, mystique, and irresistible erotic presence • Activates the parasympathetic nervous system, telling your body you are safe to feel good.• Aligns you with your inner siren archetype: fluid, wild, enchanting • Supports erotic healing: softening after trauma, harshness, or fear • Helps you attract partners who value passion, depth, and devotion • Strengthens your ability to receive pleasure fully.

#29. Sex Worker Prayer — pg. 60 • Enhances erotic dignity, financial magnetism, and boundary power • Attracts respectful, generous, high-quality clients or admirers • Increases personal safety, intuitive awareness, and energetic shielding • Strengthens the confidence needed for erotic labor, seduction, or public feminine expression • Removes shame, fear, or stigma around erotic self-expression • Amplifies beauty, allure, presence, and sensual influence • Supports financial abundance through erotic or creative skills • Balances sacred & sensual energies so you stay empowered, not drained

26 PUSSY PRAYER

SIGIL

Suggested Use:

- *During full or new moon rituals, especially those focused on release, power, or sensual embodiment.*
- *Before or after self-pleasure, womb healing, or mirror work.*
- *As a daily devotional to affirm your body as sacred space.*
- *In women's circles, sensual workshops, or rites of passage.*
- *As a boundary-clearing invocation before intimacy or partner ritual.*
- *Write this prayer's sigil, place on altar, or whisper as daily affirmations for empowerment.*

PREFACE

For too long, the feminine center has been silenced, policed, dismissed, or objectified. This piece is a proclamation.

It is the voice of a womxn who knows that her body is holy ground. This prayer is a map back to your inner altar. The Affirmed Pussy Prayer is a reminder that your sensuality is not separate from your spirituality. This is for the womxn who is done apologizing for being powerful. For being soft.

For being sacred and sensual at once.

This prayer is best experienced unrushed, unfiltered, and unapologetically embodied.

PRAYER

1. Pussy. Yoni. Portal. Garden. Goddess. Center of creation, Seat of wisdom, pulse of pleasure, the great doorway between spirit and form. I bow, in awe, in song, in reverence, in gratitude.
2. Pussy, my pussy, is a portal: to spirit, to power, to creation itself, the roadway to the heart.
3. She is the gateway through which life enters and the fountain through which honey flows.
4. Holy is this gate of life, this soft and powerful Center of Creation, Sanctuary of Pleasure, well of intuition, keeper of blood mysteries and primal knowing, I honor you.
5. May you be met with reverence, touched with consciousness, honored as the altar that you are.
6. You are the first home of every soul, the moon-rhythm in the flesh, the divine embodied.

7. Sweet Yoni, only those who come in exaltation may enter the sanctuary.
Only those who recognize the omnipotent may be received.
Only those who honor the heart, the energy, and the spirit
are permitted to touch what is divine.
8. My dearest garden, you are the first language, the first altar, the first God.
9. In your folds are mantras.
In your wetness, anointing.
In your pleasure, prophecy.
10. Here there is no repentance, no cowering.
11. Here we are alive, luminous and limitless.
12. The Pussy is the priestess.
The body is the sanctuary.
My surrender to Goddess is the offering.
And I, I am the psalm.
So it is.

SENSUAL SOUL

SIGIL

Suggested Use:

- ***Use it to reconnect with your sensual energy, reignite self-appreciation, and restore the flow between body, spirit, and emotion.***
- ***In the morning to start your day feeling magnetic and grounded.***
- ***Before sensual movement, creative work, or intimacy.***
- ***When reconnecting with your body after a period of stress, numbness, or disconnection.***
- ***During Venus hours (Fridays, dawn, or dusk) for amplified energy.***
- ***As a ritual of devotion to yourself, when no one else is watching, and the moment is yours.***

PREFACE

Sensuality is one of the soul's ways of feeling God through the body. It's one of life's most vivid, conscious experiences. It roots us in our body, our breath, our senses, and reminds us we are fully alive. This Spiritist prayer calls upon the energy of Divine Delight as a symbol of divine feminine beauty, attraction, and creative flow. It surrounds you with the frequency of delight and draws you back into your body to be celebrated. Speak this aloud when you feel disconnected from your sensual nature.

When you want to remember your beauty, your magnetism, your glow.

PRAYER

1. We do not find the divine by escaping this flesh, but by reading its sacred scripture. We do not transcend the flesh to find grace; we meet it within the flesh's own fire.
2. Let the flesh be the proof, the undeniable evidence that we are here, and that to be here is to be blessed, a temporary, terrible, and beautiful sacrament of touch.
3. May Divine Delight pour from the stars above, reminding me that I am made of brilliance.
4. Divine Delight stands to my right, guiding my action with euphoria.
5.Divine Delight stands to my left, guarding my heart with ease.
6. Divine Delight is before me, opening paths of passion and connection.
7. Divine Delight is behind me, blessing my past and steadying my steps.
8. Divine Delight is within me, alive in every breath, every touch, every pulse of desire.

9. I am a spirit clothed in form, a divine womxn dancing in the waves of splendor, a living force of deep love and creative power.
10. I welcome sensuality as real nourishment.
11. I receive pleasure as devotion.
12. I honor my body as a living space of connection, felicity, and manna.
13. May my energy attract what uplifts.
May my presence awaken what is real.
May my soul remember that delight is my natural rhythm.
So it is.

COMPANION SENSUALITY PRAYER

COSMIC INVOCATION OF SACRED SENSUALITY

Infinite Source of Pleasure and Vibration awaken the cosmos within this body.

I am no stranger to ecstasy.

I am a child of the Big Bang's primal sigh,a vessel of celestial fire.

Every nerve ending is a star.

Every heartbeat is a drum calling creation into form.

My body is not separate from the divine, it is the divine, experiencing itself as sensation.

Let my voice find the frequency that makes planets dance.

I summon a sensuality that is sacred as the pulse of life.

May my walk be a gravitational wave.

May my touch be a quantum entanglement.

May my presence be an event horizon, drawing all that is beautiful, pleasurable, and life-affirming into my orbit.

I claim this pleasure without shame or apology.

For to be sensual is to be in constant, joyful conversation with creation itself.

And so it is.

THE GOSPEL OF PLEASURE

SIGIL

__Suggested Use:__

- *Create a pleasure altar with flowers, fruit, candles, and perfume, then read aloud.*
- *Journal about what pleasure means to you after reading the prayer.*
- *Read the prayer whenever you catch yourself withholding joy from yourself.*
- *Recite during Venus hours on Friday as a rite of beauty, pleasure, and self-worth.*
- *Before intimate encounters.*

PREFACE

Pleasure has been misunderstood.
Many were taught to approach it with suspicion, to ration it, to earn it through sacrifice, or to place it at the edges of a worthy life.
These words invite a return to the feast of life.
They speak to the womxn who has spent years surviving and now desires to thrive. To the womxn who is learning that softness and power can share the same throne. To the womn reclaiming her capacity to receive without guilt, to savor without apology, and to experience life with her whole heart.

PRAYER

1. I decree that pleasure is an honored guest within the temple of my being.
2.The Divine hid nectar within the flower, wine in the grape, and ecstasy in the living body. Nothing so beautiful arrived here by mistake.
3. I shall no longer approach pleasure as a beggar. I shall return to it as a daughter returning home. For the Holy did not place rivers of delight within creation only to forbid their flow.
4. I drink deeply from the cup of ecstasy, whose sweet medicine revives my spirit as I partake in the feast of being alive.
5. I decree pleasure as holy and restorative.
I decree that pleasure is a nutrient.
For the spirit grows fat on pleasure before it ever kneels.
6. I shall not make a virtue of deprivation
while abundance stands at my door,
her hand raised, her basket full.
7. Pleasure loosens the jaw where sorrow hides itself and unbinds the belly where fear makes its nest.

8. I dissolve every voice that taught me to fear my own aliveness.
For no good shall come from denying myself of delight.
9. I decree: My hand learns to receive without guilt.
This hand breaks a curse older than my grandmother's name,
older than the first mother's shame. To receive without apology is to uncurl the fist that held the bloodline tight.
10. I open myself to sacred pleasure, openly receive sweetness as blessing and ecstasy as communion.
11. For I was not created merely to endure.
I was created to experience the fullness of life.
12.I offer myself as living testament to the generosity of the Divine.
13. And every joy I receive becomes a hymn of gratitude sung through my soul.
14. Pleasure nourishes me.
Pleasure awakens me.
Pleasure reminds me that I belong to life.
15. I welcome pleasure.
So it is.

COMPANION SIREN PRAYERS

SIREN AWAKENING

Great Mother of the deep and rising tide,
I call upon the Siren within me, as a liberator of women and of every soul who has been told to be small, to be quiet, to be convenient.
Great Mother, let this energy move through me now. I carry no malice. I hold no hunger for power over another.
I am here to free:
to free myself from the cage of "too much,"
to free myself from the leash of "not enough,"
to free myself from the endless performance of palatability.
I am inconvenient when convenience is a cage. I vocalize the wave's rhythm.
Let the Siren's energy walk with me today,
in my stride, my stillness, my silence, my song.
And when I lie down tonight, let her ebb gently, leaving me not empty, but deeply washed.
I call the souls of the settled world, I sing to any drought in my spirit, offering a necessary flood.
For I am a servant of the abyss, a keeper of the mysteries that can only be felt when the noise of the world is washed away.

SEX WORKER PRAYER

FOR WEALTH, GENEROSITY, & SACRED EXCHANGE

SIGIL

<u>Suggested Use:</u>

- ***Speak this prayer in the morning before starting your workday to open your channels for abundance.***
- ***Repeat before meeting with clients, collaborators, or partners to align the energy toward generosity and fair exchange.***
- ***Light a gold or green candle while reciting the prayer to amplify its wealth-attracting frequency.***
- ***Keep it as part of your prosperity altar or journal and recite it regularly to strengthen your connection to the flow of wealth.***

PREFACE

The Sex Worker Prayer for Wealth, Generosity, and Sacred Exchange is a spiritualist affirmation of abundance, reciprocity, and divine flow. It acknowledges money, gifts, and resources as sacred energies moving through the universe in alignment with love, gratitude, and mutual respect. It is especially potent for those whose work is rooted in beauty, connection, or creative expression, and who seek to attract generosity while maintaining self-worth and dignity.

PRAYER

1. Divine Mothers of Prosperity and Pleasure,
I open myself to receive the currency of generosity and wealth that is meant for me.
2. I call forth men and women whose hearts are open and whose hands are generous.
3. I attract patrons, sponsors, and providers who honor the magnitude of my presence and my worth.
4. May those drawn to me find bliss in caring for me, in giving freely to bless my life, in funding my greatest dreams and fulfilling my desires.
5. I welcome fortune in all forms: money, gifts, luxuries, and the security I deserve.
6. Every soul I meet feels compelled to give to me, to provide for me with love, excitement, and adoration.
7. I am magnetic to wealth, and those who desire me express their desire through generosity without limit.
My existence is a great gift from the Divine that allows me a life of comfort, prosperity, and ease.

8. I am worthy of being cared for, safe, supported, and adorned.
9.The more I receive, the more my gratitude grows and the more I am blessed in return.
10. I live in the current of opulence, and in this current I am always provided for.
11. Wrap me in a cloak of Your protection as I walk through the valley of the shadow.
12. Guard my body from harm, my mind from despair, and my spirit from corrosion.
13. Give me the wisdom of a serpent to navigate danger, and the gentleness of a dove to protect my heart.
14. I release the shame that the world tries to place upon me, for I am a beloved child of the Divine. I claim my right to safety, to respect, and to a life of my own choosing.
15. May the Light that sees me, bless me.
The Strength that sustains me, empower me.
The Love that created me, heal me.
And may I walk forward, one step at a time, into a dawn of my own making.
So it is.

COMPANION PRAYER FOR SEX WORK & WEALTH

SPOKEN CHARM FOR WEALTH & GENEROSITY

I am magnetic to wealth and generosity.
Those who desire me give freely, joyfully, and without limit.
I am worthy of every gift, every blessing, every love offering.
Gold and gifts, they freely give,
I thrive, I shine, I love, I live."

PROSPERITY CHARM

I claim prosperity without shame.
Money flows to me like rivers to the ocean, no longer as wages for my worth,
but as reciprocal honor for my sacred labor.
My hands are open, my rates are divine law.

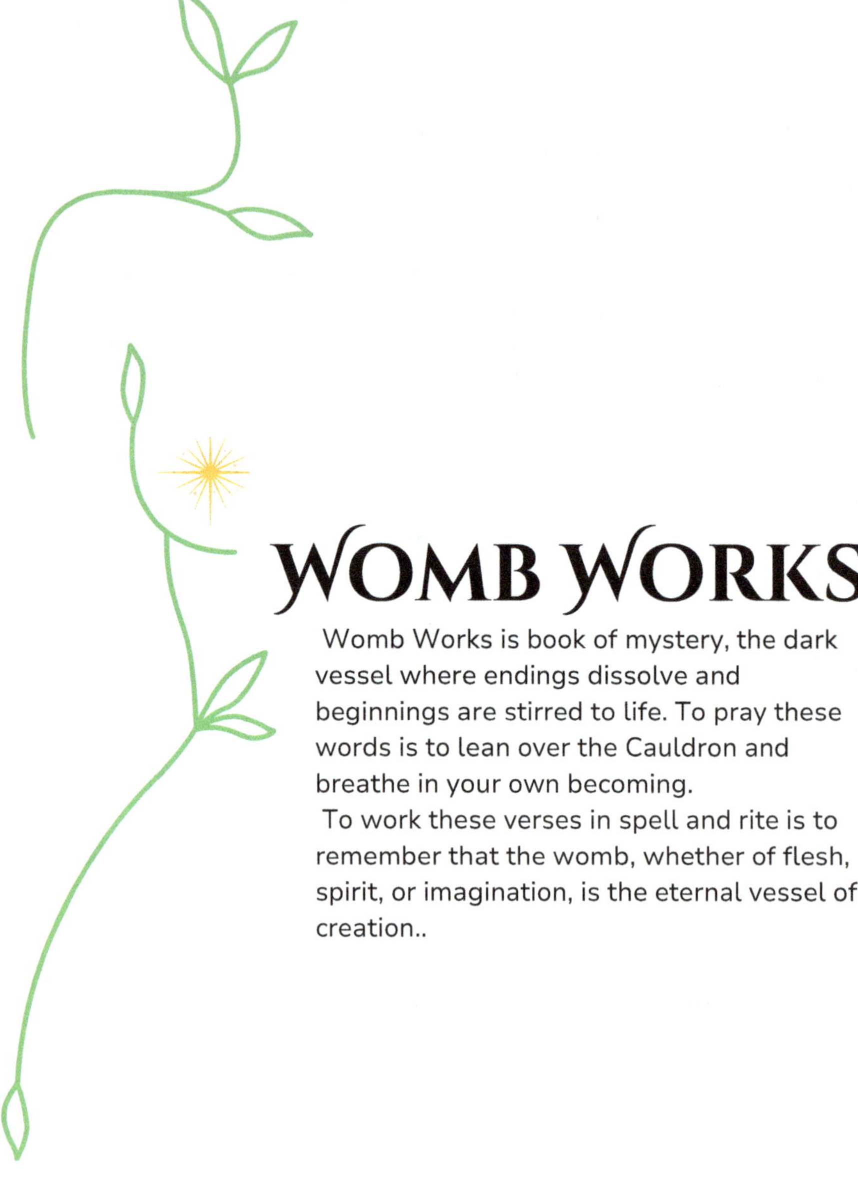

WOMB WORKS

Womb Works is book of mystery, the dark vessel where endings dissolve and beginnings are stirred to life. To pray these words is to lean over the Cauldron and breathe in your own becoming.

To work these verses in spell and rite is to remember that the womb, whether of flesh, spirit, or imagination, is the eternal vessel of creation..

The Dissertation of Womb Works

Womxn learned early to live from the neck up, to think her way through a world that rarely asked her to feel. But beneath the ribs, beneath the noise, there was always a quieter knowing, an ancient warmth that speaks in tides and cycles.
Your womb-space is a living archive. It holds not only the genetic memory of your ancestry but **soul memory.**

The womb being more than an organ of the body, it should be exalted as a holy space, a living sanctuary where spirit and matter first learn to recognize one another. Across cultures, lineages, and mystical traditions, the womb has been understood not merely as a place of reproduction, but as the seat of feminine wisdom, intuition, memory, and creation itself.
Spiritually, the womb functions as an inner altar. It is a place where intention gathers, where emotion is held, and where unseen forces are shaped into form. Even in bodies that do not menstruate, conceive, or carry children, the womb remains active as a center of creative and intuitive power.
The womb is where life is received before it is expressed. Just as the earth holds the seed in darkness before the sprout breaks the surface, the womb holds ideas, desires, grief, visions, and futures before they emerge into the world. This is why the womb is often sensitive to emotional experience. It remembers what the mind tries to forget. It stores what the heart has not yet spoken.

To honor the spiritual nature of the womb is to understand that it responds to attention, reverence, and care. What is ignored becomes stagnant. What is feared becomes tense. What is honored begins to heal. When a womxn speaks prayers into her womb, anoints it with oil, rests it, or simply places a hand there with intention, she is communing with a sacred center of consciousness.

The womb reminds us that darkness is not absence, but simply preparation. Your power is greatest not when your womb holds a visible, physical child, but when it holds the unmanifest potential, the pure, infinite possibility before it takes form. This "empty" state is its most potent and holy aspect. In this space, you are united with the Divine Mother before the first word of creation was spoken. Honor your fallow seasons as periods of cosmic alignment and infinite potential.
You need not travel to find a sacred site. The most profound pilgrimage is the journey inward to the altar of your own womb. Sit in meditation as you would at a temple. Bring offerings of breath, gratitude, and loving attention. Listen for the oracle within. This inner shrine is ever-present, accessible, and holds the direct line to your deepest knowing.

Womb Works

ENERGETIC IMPACT
WHAT EACH PRAYER ACTIVATES.

#30. Invocation of the Red Flow — pg. 65 Releases tension, shame, or fear around bleeding • Encourages timely arrival of period • Supports flow, easing stagnation or delays
#31. Blessing for the Womb in Mourning — pg. 67 Heals grief stored in the womb after miscarriage, abortion, or loss • Rebuilding trust in the body • Gently dissolves shame, guilt, and sorrow • Restores womb vitality • Supports spiritual connection with lost or ancestral children
#32. The Womb's Rest — pg. 69 Restores depleted womb energy after abortion, birth, illness, or stress• Encourages recovery • Eases pain, fatigue, and emotional overwhelm • Supports hormonal balance through rest • Helps the womb close energetically after a rupture or release • Rebuilds foundation for creativity and fertility
#33. First Blood Rites of Passage — **pg. 71** Honors maidenhood and the 1st menstruation • Initiates power, self-worth, & body confidence • Creates reverence for cycles + transition • Heals early shame or secrecy around puberty • Opens the path of womxnhood with pride and protection • Blesses the young feminine spirit with ancestral guidance
#34. **Psalm of the Queen's Crown — pg. 73** Empowers menopausal transition as awakening, not loss • Restores pride in elderhood and feminine maturity • Strengthens identity beyond reproductive cycles • Calls in support from ancestral crones and matriarchs • Awakens intuitive + visionary abilities heightened at menopause • Brings confidence in this new life stage
#35. Song for the Child Who Dances in Heaven — pg. 75 Creates spiritual connection with a child in the ancestral realm • Provides comfort, closure, and heart-softening after loss • Honors the presence of the child's spirit with dignity • Encourages acceptance and emotional integration • Opens communication through dreamwork or signs • Helps transform sorrow into sacred remembrance
#36. Prayer for Womb Healing — pg. 77 Heals physical and emotional womb imbalances • Supports fertility, hormonal harmony • Releases trauma held in reproductive organs • Helps reconnect heart and womb energetically • Clears past lovers' energetic imprints
#37. The Sacred Womb — pg. 78 Activates the womb as spiritual portal + creative engine • Restores reverence for feminine essence • Enhances conscious fertility • Awakens divine feminine intuition • Clears patriarchal, cultural, or ancestral shame
#38. Yoni Blessing — pg. 80 • Awakens the inner goddess and feminine spirit • Strengthens intuition, receptivity, and emotional intelligence • Balances softness with strength • Heals identity wounds related to womxnhood • Restores feminine confidence and inner glow • Deepens spiritual connection to feminine source energy • Encourages heart-centered leadership and compassion • Reclaims hidden or suppressed feminine power

INVOCATION OF THE RED FLOW

A PSALM FOR HEALING THE MENSTRUAL CYCLE

SIGIL

Suggested Use:

- *Recite this psalm during your bleed or in the days leading up to it.*
- *Collect a few drops of menstrual blood (or red flower petals) and place them in a bowl of water to represent renewal. Read the psalm aloud, then pour the water into the earth or a potted plant as an offering of release and gratitude.*
- *Whisper one verse before bed to calm emotional surges or soothe PMS tension.*
- *Read this psalm when experiencing painful or irregular cycles, fatigue, or body disconnection.*

PREFACE

The reproductive system, with its cycles and mysteries, is not a burden, it's a blessing, an intimate expression of divine order and feminine wisdom. Yet when these rhythms fall out of harmony, we may feel disconnected, discouraged, or even forgotten.

This psalm is a spiritual invocation, a sacred offering for those seeking healing, balance, and restoration. Whether you are navigating irregular cycles, hormonal imbalance, or the emotional weight surrounding your body's rhythms, let this be your prayer-song.

PSALM

1. Sacred is this blood,
this ancient tide within me, a covenant, a well of ancient knowing.
2. Holy is this monthly release, this primal prayer of my body. I honor its rhythm. I bless its purpose.
3. To the womb that contracts and cleanses,
be at ease.
4. To the heart that feels deeply, be held.
5. To the spirit that withdraws, be honored.
6. This body is fulfilling its wisdom.
7. I now release all inherited shame, all stories of impurity, all undertones of weakness.
8. I let go of comparisons, of calendars, of expectations.
9. Where there has been pain, I invite ease.
10. Where there has been frustration, I invite flow. My blood knows what to do.
It has known since the first mother bled into the river and called it prayer. I step aside.
I let the ancient wisdom rise.

11. Blessed be the inner winter, the time of rest and revelation.
Blessed be the inner spring, the quickening of new clarity.
Blessed be the inner summer, the radiant peak of power.
Blessed be the inner autumn, the wise and winding down.
Each phase holds medicine. Each shift holds a message.
12. I listen. I learn. I lean in.
13. May my hormones dance in divine harmony.
14. May my blood flow like a peaceful river.
15. May my emotions be respected messengers.
16. May my cycle be a source of insight, not injury.
17. My womb is a compass. My blood is a blessing.
18. I am in partnership with this process.
So it is.

COMPANION RED FLOW PRAYER

THE COMING OF THE FLOW

Sacred Source of Life and Flow,
I come before You with an open heart and a trusting spirit.
You who set the moon to wax and wane in divine rhythm, let that same rhythm move gently through me now.
I welcome balance in my body that my cycle may align as it was designed, timely, peaceful, and whole.
If there is any block within me, physical, emotional, or spiritual, I release it into Your healing light.
Let my womb awaken in its time.
Let my blood flow when it is ready.
Let my body move in tune with the holy pulse of creation.
I do not fear delay; I welcome harmony.
I call upon divine order, upon nature's wisdom and upon the spirit of restoration.
Let all systems within me work together for my highest good.
Thank You for hearing me, for holding me, and for reminding me that I am aligned with the sacred flow of life.
So be it.

BLESSING FOR THE WOMB IN MOURNING

A PRAYER OF CLOSURE AFTER MISCARRIAGE

FOR THOSE WHO WILL BEAR NO MORE CHILDREN

SIGIL

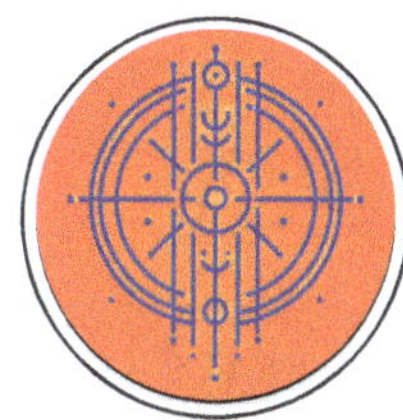

Suggested Use:

- *On a new moon, to symbolize release and renewal.*
- *On the anniversary of your miscarriage or a due date that never came.*
- *When you feel lingering sorrow, guilt, or emotional weight.*
- *When you are ready to consciously close the doorway to future pregnancies.*
- *Write a letter to your body or to the spirit of the child.*
- *Gently anoint your belly or heart with rose or lavender oil.*

PREFACE

There is a kind of grief that lives in the body before it ever finds words.
And there is a kind of love that never fades, even when the future we imagined does.
This prayer is for the womxn who has walked the path of loss and chosen, with strength and clarity, not to walk it again.
This is a prayer of quiet power, of acceptance without regret, of remembrance without longing.
You are still whole.
You are still creative.
You are still sacred.
Let this prayer be a gentle doorway, from one version of yourself into the next.

PRAYER

1. Great Spirit, Divine Mother,
I come to You with a quiet heart,
holding the tender ache of what could have been and the sacred peace of what now is.
2. I bless the life that stirred within me, however briefly, and I bless the love that remains, forever real, even without a name, even without a cradle.
3. Though my womb may no longer be called to carry, my spirit still holds the power to create, to nurture, to give life in other sacred forms.
4. I am still a vessel of love. I am still whole.
5. I release myself from the weight of expectation.
6. I choose peace, free from pressure.
7. I honor the longing without letting it lead, and I welcome the insight this path has given me.
8. To the child I did not meet in this world:
you are woven into my memory like moonlight in water, seen, felt, and carried forward with love.

9. May I live now with soft strength, with open hands and an open heart.
10. May I find beauty in new beginnings, even those I did not expect.
11. This chapter closes not in bitterness but in reverence.
12. Let this pain soften me, not harden me.
Let it connect me to other healing hearts.
Let it make my compassion deeper, my presence kinder.
So it is.

COMPANION PRAYERS FOR CLOSURE

THE RELEASE

Great Mother, I release this dream gently back to Your keeping.
I release the guilt that asks "why?",
the anger that cries "unfair!", the body that whispers "I failed."
These are not my fictions to carry.
I let them go into Your compassionate light.

THE BLESSING OF THE JOURNEY

Though my arms are empty, my soul has been marked by this love.
Bless the tiny spirit that chose me, if only for a moment.
May their journey be peaceful, their essence wrapped in grace,
their memory a quiet star in the constellation of my life.

These prayers do not rush healing.
They simply hold space for it.
There is no timeline for this sorrow.
Your grief is valid. Your love is real.

THE WOMB'S REST

ABORTION PRAYER

SIGIL

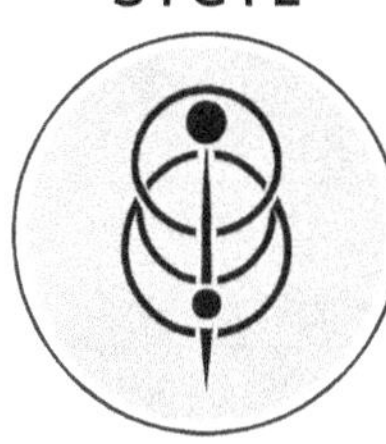

Suggested Use:

- ***During moments of regret, shame, or self-doubt.***
- ***As part of a self-healing or shadow work ritual.***
- ***After journaling about past mistakes or emotional pain.***
- ***During meditation or before sleep to release the day's weight.***
- ***In preparation for new beginnings or life changes.***
- ***After the prayer, write a note of forgiveness to yourself, read it aloud, and place it somewhere safe as a reminder of your commitment to self-love.***
- ***Draw sigil on womb with rose water for womb healing.***

PREFACE

This prayer is for women who seek spiritual healing after the deep and complex grief of ending a pregnancy. It acknowledges the reality of pain, regret, and self-judgment, while inviting the compassionate presence of the Divine Mother, a source of unconditional love, mercy, and restoration.

This prayer is not about erasing the past, but about releasing the heaviness it leaves behind. It is a pathway toward self-forgiveness, connection with the Divine, and trust that both the child's spirit and the mother's soul are held in eternal love.

PRAYER

1. Divine Mother of Mercy, who grants us free will and deep knowing, I stand before you in my fictions.
2. I honor the choice I made, a choice born of circumstance, of sacred responsibility.
3. I release all shame into your compassionate light. My decision is valid. My heart is worthy of peace.
4. Divine Spirit, I come before You with my heart laid bare, carrying the weight of a choice that has left deep sorrow in my soul.
5. I bring my pain, my grief, my confusion, and my longing for healing.
6. I acknowledge that I acted in fear and desperation, unable to see the road ahead, unable to believe I could walk it. I made a choice I cannot undo, and I now live with the ache it has left behind.
7. To the potential that briefly touched my life, I acknowledge you with love. I release you with grace.

8. May your essence return to the boundless ocean of love from which all life comes.
9. May you be wrapped in light, and may I be wrapped in peace. We are both held in the same eternal compassion.
10. Divine Mother, teach me to honor the lessons of my path without being bound by its pain. Help me rise again, carrying not only my loss but also my renewed devotion to life.
11. My life is my own. My choices are sacred.
Free from the need to justify my path to any soul but my own, I trust my wisdom. I honor my journey.
12. I thank the divine love that does not judge, but liberates.
13. I thank my spirit for its resilience.
14. I thank my body for its strength.
15. I walk forward with compassion for myself and trust in the path I have chosen.
16. I give myself permission to release, to recover, and to thrive.
So it is.

COMPANION THE WOMB'S REST PRAYER

SELF-FORGIVENESS ABORTION DECREE

I now release all shame, guilt, and self-condemnation.
I free myself from the weight of my past choices.
I embrace the truth that I am worthy of love, healing, and redemption.
I claim the light of my own compassion.
I graciously receive the lessons I have learned.
I allow my mistakes to transform into wisdom.
I forgive myself fully, completely, and without condition.
I forgive the self I once was, the self I am now, and the self I am becoming.
I reclaim my power from every story of unworthiness.
I move forward now in peace, with a clear mind and an open heart.
I am restored. I am refreshed. I am free.

1ST BLOOD RITES OF PASSAGE

PRAYER FOR FIRST MENSES. A CELEBRATION OF LIFE

SIGIL

<u>Suggested Use:</u>

- *Read this prayer aloud during a first moon ceremony, in the quiet of a private moment, or shared within a circle of trusted women.*
- *Speak it not only to the young one crossing into womxnhood, but also to the inner child within us all, who still longs to be told: You are sacred. You are whole. You are ready.*
- *As part of a mother–daughter bonding ritual.*
- *In women's circles, especially those focused on menstrual education, rites of passage, or intergenerational healing.*
- *To reclaim your own first menstrual experience through spiritual reflection and rewriting.*

PREFACE

The first period is more than a physical change. It is a spiritual doorway, a quiet yet powerful crossing from childhood into a new phase of becoming. In many cultures, this moment is honored, remembered, and celebrated as a rite of passage. This prayer was written to reclaim that sacredness, to speak blessings where there may have been embarrassment, to affirm power where there may have been confusion. It is a spiritist offering, connecting the wisdom of the ancestors, the rhythm of the Earth, and the light of the soul.

PRAYER

1. Today, your body has spoken an ancient story. You are now a keeper of rhythms, a vessel of creative power, a living bridge between spirit and earth.
2. Welcome. This blood is holy and this change is sacred.
3. You belong to yourself in a new way today.
4. This flow is never created as a curse; it is a covenant with life itself.
It is the same power that grows forests, turns tides and paints the sky at dawn.
5. Your body now holds the rhythm of the moon and the wisdom of your grandmothers.
6. May you always remember your blood is clean. Your body is wise.
7. May your cycles be gentle teachers.
May your cramps be mild, your heart light.
May you never feel shame for this natural magic. May you learn to listen to your body's deep knowing, when to rest, when to create, when to rise in your power.
8. You are entering a sisterhood of strength.
We are here for you. Always.

9. Let this day be marked with joy.
10. You are not "becoming a womxn".
You are deepening into the womxn you have always been.
11. We celebrate you.
We honor you. We bless the path you walk
and the life you may one day choose to nurture, or not.
12. The choice, like your body, is yours.
13. Go forward knowing you carry within you
the power to create, to intuit, to feel deeply, to heal, to lead, and to love fiercely.
14. This blood is your birthright, not something to hide but a reminder of the divine force you embody.
So it is.

PSALM OF THE QUEEN'S CROWN

THE WISE WOMXN: A SACRED HYMN FOR MENOPAUSE

SIGIL

Suggested Use:

- *Creative Embodiment: Dance it. Paint it. Chant it. Use it as a source of expression, your menopausal power deserves voice and movement.*
- *Circle Sharing: Bring this psalm to women's circles, menopause gatherings, or sisterhood rituals. Speak it aloud, let others echo the lines, and allow communal wisdom to rise.*
- *Mirror Work: Stand before a mirror, make eye contact with yourself, and recite the lines as personal affirmations. Let them root into your reflection.*

PREFACE

In a culture that worships youth and silences aging, menopause has been cast as an ending. But to the wise, it is the Great Turning.
This transformation is deep concentrated power.
This is the passage into the Crone, not as an old womxn cast aside, but as a Priestess of wisdom, a Keeper of stories, a living archetype, a teacher.
Let this chapter in your body's story be met with reverence, resistance has no place here.

PRAYER

1. Blessed am I in this becoming.
2. The season turns, the heated tide recedes,
no longer for the moon's bright pull I bleed.
I stand within the liminal, the space between,
what was, and what is yet to be, unseen.
3. I am the gatherer, the weaver of the tale,
the keeper of the wisdom that will never pale.
I am the hearth-fire in the community's heart,
the one who sees the whole, and not the part.
4. How could this be the end of womxnhood?
It is the unveiling of its fullness.
5. I shed the skin of who I was before to make room for the Wise One.
6. I am no longer ruled by cycles.
7. I move in spirals: wider, deeper, primal.
8. For I am grace refined. I dance where creativity becomes insight.
Nurturance becomes boundaries.
Sensitivity becomes discernment.
9. I am a tide receding to reveal a new landscape, stark and beautiful in its expression.
10.The Crone moves through me, and I hear her say: Goddess, welcome to the beyond.

11. I am the Sphinx at the gateway to the second half, keeper of the mysteries I have earned.
My body is no longer a map of fertility, let it be a chronicle of joyous survival, a testament of time.
12. My life force, once spent in a rhythm not my own, now returns to me, wholly.
13.I take up space as Priestess and a sweet, mighty torch, not as girl, nor mother.
14. The world may not understand this power, but my bones do. The ancestors sing it. The Earth beneath my feet affirms it.
15. I am stepping into the age of prophecy.
16. Let my life be a blessing, a sacred, spacious, and sovereign becoming.
17. I bless the women behind me. I summon the women ahead.
18. For I am not less. I am legend, and I am becoming more.
19. I am arriving.
So it is.

FOR THE CHILD WHO DANCES IN HEAVEN

PRAYER FOR HEALING AND HOPE OF NEW LIFE

SIGIL

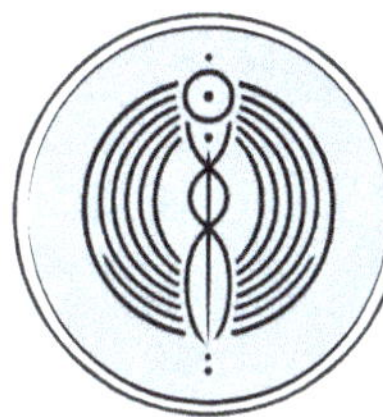

Suggested Use:

- *Read the prayer aloud or in a whisper. Let the words wash over you. If tears come, let them fall. If sorrow follows, let it speak. This prayer can be repeated as often as you need, whether daily during your grief or returned to on significant days such as anniversaries, due dates, or moments of reflection.*
- *You may read it in solitude, during a personal ritual, or with a trusted loved one or partner. Choose a time when you will not be disturbed.*
- *Create a gentle atmosphere, perhaps by lighting a candle, placing your hands on your womb, or holding a token of remembrance (such as a stone, flower, or piece of jewelry).*

PREFACE

There is a kind of love that never holds a heartbeat, yet lives forever in memory, in spirit, in subtle, the love of a mother for a soul she carried briefly, but deeply.
Miscarriage is a word often spoken clinically, but it holds a sacred weight. It is not only the loss of life; it is the loss of a dream, a possibility, a relationship with a soul who has already been loved.
This prayer is written for the womxn who has grieved in stillness, who has loved without holding. It is for the heart that longs to heal, and for the spirit that still hopes to create, to carry, and to receive life once more.

PRAYER

1.Great Mother, I come to You in quiet sorrow,
carrying the tender ache of loss.
2.The soul I carried has returned to You,
not lost, but guided home to light.
3.Though my arms are empty, my heart remains full of the love I still hold and always will.
4. Spirit of Consolation, bring peace to my body, my mind, and my heart.
5. Help me to trust in the great plan
that often moves beyond what I can see.
6. May the child I carried feel my love across the veil. May their spirit be at rest and surrounded by divine care.
7. I ask now for healing, may I never forget, but to carry this memory with softness and to transform grief into deeper compassion.
8. Beloved guides and protectors,
help me prepare my body and soul to welcome life again, whether as a physical child or as an idea brought into bloom when the time is right.

9. May the next soul who chooses me come into this world in perfect health.
10. Make this vessel ready, not replacing what was lost, but welcoming what may still come.
11. May this womb be a place of safety and serenity, a garden for new life, prepared in divine order.

So be it.
So it is.

PRAYER FOR WOMB HEALING

SIGIL

Suggested Use:

- *During physical healing from womb or reproductive issues.*
- *As part of moon cycle or fertility rituals.*
- *After womb-related surgeries or challenges.*
- *During meditation or before bedtime as a healing affirmation.*
- *In moments of self-connection and body gratitude.*
- *After the prayer, write a note of forgiveness to yourself, read it aloud, and place it somewhere safe as a reminder of your commitment to self-love.*

PREFACE

In spiritualist practice, the womb is recognized as a sacred center of creation, intuition, and deep spiritual power. It is more than a physical organ; it is an energetic vessel that holds memories, emotions, and life-force energy.

This prayer invites the healing light of the Divine Mother to restore the womb to its natural state of balance, vitality, and sacred power. By speaking it daily, you reinforce your body's natural ability to heal while also honoring the deeper spiritual connection between your physical being and the universal creative force.

DECREE

1. I now take full command of my womb space.
2. I call healing into the sanctuary of my womb.
3. This sanctuary is mine, its energy, its stories, its power. No past pain, person, or pattern has authority here.
4. I revoke all permissions for lingering harm.
5. I reclaim the womb, the cauldron, as sacred ground.
6. All stagnant energy leave now.
All stored grief, be dissolved.
All embodied trauma, be transmuted.
All cords tying me to old wounds, sever.
7. I release the sorrows buried in my flesh,
the stories of shame, the echoes of loss.
8. For every tear shall become a river of renewal, every scar a testament of strength reborn.
9. Every cell, every memory, every echo of affliction is now flooded with violet light.
10. My womb is cleared and consecrated.
11. Holy Womb, Cauldron of Creation,
now a sanctuary of power, a wellspring of intuition, from this day forward, I celebrate my womb. So it is.

THE SACRED WOMB

PSALM FOR THE BLESSING OF PREGNANCY

SIGIL

Suggested Use:

- ***To invite divine blessing for conception, fertility, and the safe, joyful arrival of a child.***
- ***During morning or evening prayer time.***
- ***Before or after fertility treatments, conception attempts, or intimate union.***
- ***During new moon or full moon fertility rituals.***
- ***While meditating with hands placed over the womb.***
- ***Pair Psalm with gentle belly massage using fertility-friendly oils such as rose, jasmine, or geranium.***
- ***Repeat daily for 21 days to build a deep energetic imprint of readiness.***

PREFACE

The Psalm for the Blessing of Pregnancy is a sacred invocation calling upon the Divine Creative Force to open the womb, strengthen the body, and prepare the heart for the miracle of new life. It draws inspiration from ancient scriptural promises of fertility, divine timing, and the generational blessing of motherhood. Spoken with faith, this psalm aligns your energy, intention, and spirit with the higher realms, creating a channel for conception to manifest in divine order.

PRAYER

1. Mother, Creator of All Beginnings,
bless my womb, and let it be a sanctuary for new life.
2. I open my body, my heart, and my home to the possibility of creation.
3. Align my rhythm with the universe's holy timing.
4. Like the earth in spring, let my body awaken, every cycle a prayer, every ovulation a sacred yes.
5. Little one, we have not yet met, but you are already loved.
6. You are a prayer made flesh, an intention taking form.
7. I quiet every voice of fear, every whisper of "not enough."
8. Let conception be an act of love, not a transaction of tension.
9. My lineage of mothers stands with me,
their strength in my blood, their resilience in my bones.

10. Great Spirit, prepare me: to carry with gallantry, to nurture with wisdom, to welcome with wild, untamed love.
11. Spirits of Mother-Love, be with me now. Counsel my steps and soften my fears.
12. My hormones dance in divine order.
13. My cells align with life's blueprint.
14. My arms already ache to hold what Heaven has promised.
15. I release anxiety. I release control.
16. I trust in a plan greater than my own.
17. Whether through my body or by another path, motherhood will find me.
18. My heart is already a cradle.
My love is already fertile ground.
So be it.

A YONI BLESSING

SIGIL

Suggested Use:

- ***Before meditation, sensual movement, or ritual work.***
- ***Prior to intimacy to deepen connection with self and partner.***
- ***During moon rituals or yoni-healing/steaming practices.***
- ***When seeking to reclaim personal power, confidence, or sensuality.***
- ***In moments of self-doubt, disconnection, or creative block.***
- ***Place your hands over your womb or heart and speak the prayer aloud with conviction.***
- ***Recite before moments of Self-Pleasure, enhancing Sex magick.***

PREFACE

In spiritualist traditions, the womb, yoni, and heart are honored as sacred gateways to divine connection, creative force, and intuitive knowing. This prayer affirms the body as holy, the feminine as powerful, and sensuality as a natural expression of the soul's truth. It is both a declaration of self-love and a call to release fear, shame, and societal conditioning that may have dimmed one's expression. By reciting it with intention, you invite your inner Goddess to rise fully grounded, radiant, and unafraid to embody her pleasure, her voice, and her divine essence.

PRAYER

1.She is my center of creation.
2. Yoni, sacred seat of the Goddess,
I honor you as the root of revelation.
3. I honor the divinity between my thighs,
with the tenderness of a blessing, the strength of a vow, a vortex of vitality, creating and craving in ecstatic turns.
4. Utterly profound, you are.
5. You choose what enters your springs.
You discern what serves your spirit.
6. Your pleasure is prayer.
7. Your boundaries are divine law.
8. You are the throne of my autonomy,
the unyielding ground of my I AM.
9. I welcome the full expression of myself,
my voice, my movement, my pleasure, my desires, without tension, without apology.
10. Sweet Yoni,
I need not look to the sky to find the Divine.
She resides here.

11. I vow to tend to you with reverence.
12. You who are the cradle of humanity.
13. You are a universe of sensation, a map of stars, a gateway of life and bliss.
14. I anoint you with praise, for you are the holiest manna.
15. Let no man, no myth, no fear distort your sacredness.
16. I bless my yoni, my womb, my body, my spirit.
I claim my right to pleasure, to presence, to playfulness.
I live as the Goddess that I am.

So it is.

COMPANION YONI PRAYERS

Speak it slowly while placing your hands over your womb or yoni.
Repeat each couplet 3-9 times, feeling the words resonate in your body.
You can hum or sway with it, turning it into a sensual movement meditation.

PUSSY BLESSING CHANT

From your depths, life emerges.
From your darkness, vision is born.
You are the portal between worlds, where spirit becomes form, and form returns to spirit.
I will celebrate your power as a dear gift.
From this day forward, I reverence you.
I respect you.
I remember you.

LOVE

Love is the root of all magic. It binds families, draws friendships, stirs passion, heals grief, and carries us back to ourselves. Within these verses are prayers that call the heart open, protect the bonds we hold dear, and draw affection like a magnet. Book of Love verses speak to the many faces of love , the warmth of friendship, the loyalty of kin, the tenderness of self-embrace, and the fierce pull of soulmates.

Love

ENERGETIC IMPACT
WHAT EACH PRAYER ACTIVATES.

#39. Awakened Heart — pg. 84 • Softens protective walls and restores your ability to give and receive love without collapsing into old wounds. • Gently dissolves suspicion, defensiveness, and protection patterns developed from old harm • Amplifies magnetic, heart-centered presence• Teaches the heart to stay open without losing discernment, creating a balanced feminine power.
#40, Everywhere I Go, I Am Loved — pg. 86 • Amplifies social magnetism + charm • Softens the energy you carry so people feel safe with you • Draws kindness and favor from strangers and acquaintances • Heals loneliness by creating constant connection energy • Helps you feel supported in every space• Encourages affection from friends, family, and partners
#41. Call of True Love — pg. 87 • Attracts soulmate-level or spiritually aligned partnerships • Strengthens existing unions with devotion + clarity • Clears emotional interference blocking true love • Creates a magnetic field that pulls compatible partners
#42. Psalm of Self-Love — pg. 89 • Activates Deep Nervous System Regulation. • Dissolves the victim mentality. • Activates Internal Validation •Development of unshakable resilience & courage • Declaration of self-worthiness.
#43. A Returning Dawn — pg. 91 • Gently pulls you out of internal darkness, softening the weight that sits on the chest and spirit. • Clears mental fog + stagnation • Helps clear spiritual darkness • Encourages you to take small steps forward, especially when you feel frozen, drained, or disconnected. • Restores hope after long sorrow
#44. Stewardship of the Temple — pg. 93 • Rebuilding body trust, reconnecting after trauma, or healing body-image wounds. • Detoxes stagnant emotional + physical energy • Increases energy and vitality • Shifts weight loss from "fixing flaws" to honoring the temple • Heals the relationship with the physical form
#45. Invocation for the Sacred Self — pg. 94 • Strengthens self-love as the root of all relationship healing • Attracts partners who resonate with your authenticity • Removes insecurity + emotional instability in love • Heightens intuition about romantic choices • Creates emotional boundaries that protect the heart • Helps you show up fully and confidently in love
#46. The Great Covenant — pg. 96 • Strengthens loyalty, trust, and relational integrity • Protects unions from interference or confusion • Deepens commitment between partners • Encourages long-term partnership building• Helps couples move as a team rather than in conflict • Calls in divine guardianship over relationships
#47. Decree of Reconciliation — pg. 98 • Opens pathways for forgiveness after conflict • Clears misunderstandings between partners or loved ones • Restores warmth in emotionally strained connections • Helps dissolve pride, tension, and emotional walls • Encourages honest communication + heart-centered repair • Supports reunions when aligned with divine timing

AWAKENED HEART

A SCRIPTURE FOR SHE WHO HOLDS AN OPEN HEART

SIGIL

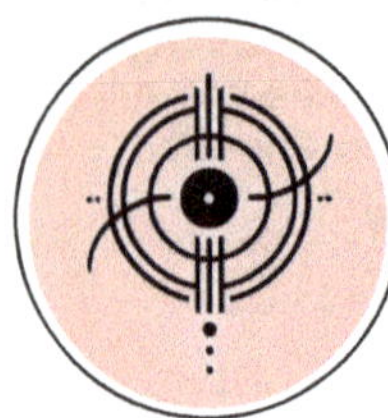

<u>Suggested Use:</u>

- *Place your hand over your heart at sunrise and speak the verse to reopen emotional pathways after hurt.*
- *Speak to soften emotional tension and open your day with love.*
- *Repeat this verse facing east at dawn or under moonlight to heal love wounds.*
- *Recite while holding a rose quartz or while journaling your desires for love, connection, or abundance.*
- *When setting a goal, lightly tap your heart's center like a tuning fork calling in softness.*

PREFACE

In a world that often prizes the closed fist of control, the shielded heart of skepticism, and the relentless pursuit of external validation, this scripture calls you back to your innate architecture. The feminine principle, in harmony with Nature, teaches us that the deepest strength lies in intelligent openness. Here, an "open heart" is redefined as a sacred instrument of transformation and a magnetic field of aligned attraction.

PRAYER

1. Her heart is not merely a chamber of flesh, but the sanctuary of the Self. A heart that is closed is a temple door locked, where the divine guest stands outside.
2. The feminine spirit, aligned with nature, knows this truth: the seed must split open to receive the rain. The womb must be empty to host life. The chalice must be open upward to be filled.
3.Therefore, let the gates of the heart swing wide. Let them be open to the dawn whose light dispels the shadows of fear. Let them be open to the moon, whose cool nectar soothes the burns of past wounding.
4. An open heart is not without boundaries; it is guided by discernment, receiving what is pure and transforming all else through awareness.
5. With an open heart, you attract in harmony. Like resonates with like. Your open heart will call forth relationships, creations, and abundance that match its own frequency, consciousness, bliss.

6. With an open heart, you lead from receptivity. Your power is not in pushing against, but in knowing when to receive, when to nurture, and when to release, as the earth knows the season for each.
7. This is the supreme feminine strength: the courage to feel fully, to receive deeply, and to love from a source that is eternally replenished by ultimate Reality.
8. May your heart be as open as the sky, holding clouds of emotion without being torn by them.
9. May your heart be as deep as the ocean, receiving all rivers of experience without losing its stillness.
10. May your heart be as bright as the sacred flame, receiving the offering of each moment and transforming it into light.
11. Therefore, beloved one, tend to the openness of your heart as the master gardener tends the most precious rose. Prune the thorns of bitterness, water it with tears of release, and let it bask in the sun of unconditional love. For from this garden, your whole life shall bloom.
So it is.

COMPANION AWAKENED HEART PRAYER

LOVE AS A DANCE
DANCE AS OFFERING

Beloved of my soul, Goddess, All that is
I dance to vanish into You.
I dance to dissolve.
I dance to be drawn upward, inward, beyond form.
I dance until there is no dancer, only the dance itself.
I dance because rhythm heals what words cannot reach.
I dance to remember euphoria, to remember freedom, to remember myself.
When I dance, I shake free of sorrow and awaken to the Goddess within.
Sound becomes my medicine. Movement becomes my prayer.
O Divine Presence,
Take my movement as offering.
Take my movement as devotion.
Take this body and make it Yours.
Dear ones, let us anoint this earth with dance.
Let our feet write love into the ground.
I am pleasure in motion.
I am love in motion.
So it is.

EVERYWHERE I GO, I AM LOVED DECREE

SIGIL

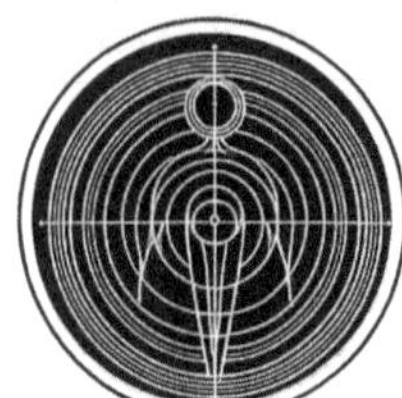

Suggested Use:

- ***Speak this decree aloud upon waking to set the tone of your day and infuse yourself with magnetic energy.***
- ***Before Social Gatherings or Meetings, repeat to draw in loving, supportive, and favorable interactions.***
- ***Whisper or chant the key line, "Everywhere I go, I am loved," whenever you step into a new space.***
- ***Write the decree in your journal and pair it with a candle, crystal (rose quartz or garnet), or incense to anchor the energy.***

PREFACE

This decree is crafted for those who wish to embody love as their natural state and attract it everywhere they go. It affirms your divine worth and activates your magnetic energy, making your presence one of warmth, respect, and admiration. By aligning with the frequency of love, you carry it as a living aura that others feel and respond to instantly. This decree is a reminder that love is not something you chase, it is who you are, and from that embodiment, it flows toward you abundantly.

DECREE

1. Divine Source of Love,
I awaken my heart as a living beacon of beauty, glamour, and glee.
2. Everywhere I go, love recognizes me.
Everywhere I go, favor surrounds me.
Everywhere I go, hearts open to receive me.
3. I am surrounded by a love that does not fail. It is the ground beneath my feet and the air that fills my lungs.
4. My words are wrapped in honey, my spirit shines with incandescence, and my energy is magnetic to love in all its forms, romantic, platonic, divine, and communal.
5. Love does not depend on my perfection, but on my existence. I cannot wander beyond its reach, for it is the very fabric of my being.
6. I am cherished. I am adored. I am seen.
7. I am honored wherever I step, and I attract only those who reflect my radiance back to me.
8. Everywhere I go, I am loved, celebrated, and uplifted. When my mind forgets, let my bones remember: Everywhere I go, I am loved.

And so it is.

41 CALL OF TRUE LOVE

SIGIL

Suggested Use:

- *Before or after journaling on love, relationships, or emotional healing.*
- *When releasing past relationships and clearing space for new connection.*
- *Any time you feel ready to align your energy with true, reciprocal love.*
- *During a heart-opening ritual or self-love ceremony.*
- *Speak it slowly and clearly. Let each word soften your heart, energize your spirit, and open your field to loving connection.*
- *Use this prayer after releasing past heartbreak or trauma, affirming that you are ready for new love.*
- *Repeat the prayer daily until you feel fully aligned with the love you seek, then continue weekly or during the new moon to amplify your magnetism.*

PREFACE

Love is more than an emotional desire. Love is a vibration, a divine force that draws us into deeper alignment with ourselves and others. To call in true love is not to chase or plead, but to create space within the heart where love can land, thrive, and be honored.

This prayer is for those who have done the work of healing and now feel the sacred pull toward union. Whether you are preparing to meet your soulmate, deepening a connection already blooming, or simply reconnecting with the essence of love within yourself, this psalm serves as a spiritual mirror, reflecting the love you are now ready to receive.

PRAYER

1. Spirit of Unconditional Love,
I release all past heartache, all old patterns, all lingering attachments.
2. I forgive former loves and myself.
3. I cleanse my heart and energy field,
making space for the new, the true, the divine.
4. My past does not dictate my future.
My heart is open. My spirit is ready.
5. I am not calling for a mirror to admire my own reflection, nor a shield to hide from my own battles. I am calling for a harbor where my rest is deep, and from which we both set sail, stronger.
6. Let our paths converge in divine timing,
with ease, with bliss, with deep knowing.
7. May we see each other, and be seen, without disguise.
8. I call in a partner of integrity, depth, and kindness, whose strength is gentle, whose laughter is easy, whose heart is open to give and receive love.
9. May we be mirrors of growth,

sanctuaries of peace and partners in purpose.
Not a half seeking completion, but two wholes choosing connection.
10. By the power of love that moves stars and souls, I magnetize this union now.
11. I align my energy with the frequency of sacred partnership.
Every thought, every action, every prayer brings us closer together.
12. The cords of our spirits already entwine in the unseen.
Now, let them manifest in the seen.
13. I release this prayer into the heart of the Universe.
I trust in its wisdom. I surrender the how, the when, the where.
I focus on becoming the partner I wish to attract, loving, present, and whole.
14. I am ready. I am worthy. I am waiting with an open heart.
So it is.

42 PSALM OF SELF-LOVE

SIGIL

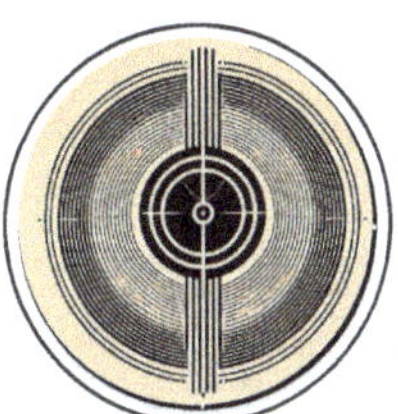

Suggested Use:

- *Select one verse that resonates with you and carry it in your mind throughout the day as a mantra or touchstone.*
- *Read it quietly before bed, replacing any self-critical thoughts from the day with the psalm's messages of acceptance and wholeness.*
- *Light a candle as a symbol of the Divine Light within you. Read the psalm in the glow of the flame, seeing it as the light of your own soul being honored.*
- *Say the prayer before sleep as an offering of gratitude to your body for what it carried you through that day, reinforcing a positive self-image.*

PREFACE

The Divine is not a distant monarch to be appeased, but an indwelling presence, the very source and substance of our being. To know the Divine is to know oneself; to love the Divine is to love the life that animates your own soul. "Psalm of self-love" is therefore an invitation to turn the timeless words of worship inward. It is a declaration that you are not separate from the goodness you seek. The green pastures, the still waters, the restored soul, these are not places to find, but truths to remember within yourself. May these words serve as a mirror, reflecting your own inherent power. Speak them or hold them in your heart as a reminder that you are the beloved, the lover, and the love, all united in the sacred temple of your own being.

PRAYER

1. The Divine is my shepherd, therefore I shall not despise my own soul. I am the sheep of Great Goddess's pasture, and also the shepherd of my own being.
2. I am led to lie down in green pastures of peace. Beside the still waters of my own heart, I am restored.
3. My soul is restored not by another, but by the breath of the Infinite that lives within me. For love's sake, I am guided on the path of righteousness, which is the path of knowing my own worth.
4. Gracefully, though I walk through the valley of self-doubt and the shadow of past failures, I will fear no evil. For the Light of the Source is with me; its truth and its comfort, they heal me.
5. I prepare a table of forgiveness before me in the presence of my inner critics. I anoint my own head with the oil of acceptance. My cup, which is my own heart, overflows with compassion for myself.

6. Let every fiber of my being praise the Source. Let my hands praise in their service, my mind praise in its thoughts of kindness toward itself, and my heart praise in its endless, unconditional embrace of who I am.
7. How precious therefore is my own being to me. How vast is the sum of my own worth. If I should count my own value, they are more in number than the sand.
8. Search me, O Light within, and know my heart. Try me and know my thoughts! And see if there be any way of self-rejection in me and lead me in the way of love everlasting.
9. I am the beloved. I am the lover. I am the love. This is the day which the Divine has made; I will rejoice and be glad in it, and in the self that I am.
So be it.
So it is.

COMPANION BODY SELF LOVE PRAYER

BLESSED BODY

Blessed is this body, my first home, my most faithful companion, the living temple that houses my eternal spirit.
Blessed are these feet that have walked me through joy and through sorrow, that have carried me toward my destiny, one step at a time.
Blessed are these legs, strong and steady, rooted like ancient trees, yet willing to bend, to kneel, to dance, to rise again.
Blessed is this womb, deep center of intuition and creation, keeper of cycles, vessel of life and letting go. May it always know its sacred worth.
Blessed is this heart, that has broken and healed, that remains soft enough to love, strong enough to forgive, and brave enough to beat on.
Blessed are these hands, that have built, held, released, and blessed. May they always create in kindness and touch with reverence.
Blessed is this voice, that speaks my truth, sings my sorrow, whispers my prayers. May it always sound like freedom.
Blessed is this skin, that feels sunlight and wind, that tells the story of my years, that wraps my soul in a tapestry of touch and sensation.
Blessed is this breath, the invisible thread connecting body to spirit, moment to moment, life to Life.
I honor this body not for how it appears, but for all it has allowed me to be, to feel, and to become. It has been my shelter in storm, my vessel of pleasure, my instrument of service, my map of memory.
Therefore, I vow to care for it with tenderness, to listen to its wisdom, to celebrate its strength, to forgive its limitations, and to thank it daily.
For this body is not separate from my soul,
it is my soul's conversation with the world.

A RETURNING DAWN

A PRAYER TO LIFT THE VEIL OF DEPRESSION

SIGIL

Suggested Use:

- *Morning or Evening Practice: Speak the prayer during quiet hours, either at sunrise when the world is still, or at night when the weight feels heaviest.*
- *Salt Bath or Foot Soak: Combine warm water with sea salt and lavender or rose oil. As you soak, imagine emotional heaviness dissolving and being held by the earth.*
- *Blanket Meditation: Wrap yourself in a soft blanket and sit quietly after the prayer, allowing yourself to simply be held, by the words, the warmth, and the Divine.*
- *Buddhist Metta Prayer – "May I be happy. May I be safe. May I be free from suffering."*

PREFACE

There are seasons when the soul feels dimmed, when joy becomes a distant echo, and even the simplest light seems unreachable. In these moments, depression is not just a feeling, but a fog that clouds every corner of life. This prayer is offered as a quiet reaching out, through the veil of darkness.

It does not ask you to be strong.

It simply invites you to turn toward something greater, compassionate, patient, luminous and ask for help.

PRAYER

1. Mother of all, enter this shadowed place within me.

2. Somewhere beneath this sorrow, deeper than the story of my failures, there is a quiet well that has not run dry.

I may not taste it today, but I will trust it is there.

3. I seek the cracks where the light gets in, however faint: The slant of afternoon sun on the floor.The kindness in a stranger's eyes.

The memory of a laugh that once felt real.

I will collect these splinters of light like sacred tinder, until there is enough to build a small fire in the dark.

4. Where darkness clings, remind me of the sun.

5. Let me remember: this heaviness is not forever, and even the longest night bows to the dawn.

6. By your presence, Spirit of Nurture,

lift me beyond the reach of despair, into the wide fields of peace, where I may walk again in the fullness of glory.

7. Take this ache, this fog that clouds my soul.
Lift it gently, like mist in morning light.
8. Where I feel numb, awaken me.
Where I feel hollow, fill me.
Where I feel lost, guide me home.
9. I no longer ask for false brightness or quick fixes.
I ask for healing that is holy, for joy that roots deep, for peace that holds me like warm hands in the dark.
10. This darkness is a season; it is a passage.
11. I have not forgotten the goodness, only misplaced it for a time.
Help me remember.
12. Place light at the edges of my days.
Let it grow, quietly, steadily, until I can feel again, until I can laugh without guilt, until I can see beauty and believe it.
13. I will carry that light for others too as a gift I was trusted to share.
So be it.
So it is.

STEWARDSHIP OF THE TEMPLE

WEIGHT LOSS & BODY REBALANCING

SIGIL

<u>Suggested Use:</u>

- *This invocation is a sacred act of reclaiming your body as your ally, not your enemy.*
- *You are beginning a new cycle of healing or transformation.*
- *You are releasing old patterns tied to food, body image, or emotional weight.*
- *You desire to reconnect with your body as sacred, wise, and worthy.*
- *You're in need of motivation rooted in self-love rather than self-punishment.*
- *Daily or weekly recitation, preferably in the morning before meals or movement.*
- *Mirror work; speak the invocation while looking into your own eyes, hand on your belly or heart.*

PREFACE

In a world where the journey to wellness is often reduced to numbers, calories counted, pounds lost, and inches shed, we forget that true transformation begins within. The body is not merely flesh and bone; it is a sacred vessel, a temple of the spirit. To heal the body, we must first nourish the soul.

May this prayer guide you toward self-love, discipline, and ease. May it remind you that every step forward is a sacred act, and every challenge is an opportunity for growth. Trust the process, lean into faith, and let your transformation be a testament to the power of spirit over struggle.

PRAYER

1. O beloved inhabitant of this holy flesh: your body is not an adversary to be conquered, but a temple of the Divine Spirit, a sacred instrument of your soul's purpose. The journey of release is not a war against self, but a homecoming to your natural state of grace and equilibrium.
2. Let every morsel that passes your lips be chosen with conscious honor. Ask: "Does this nourish the temple or merely clutter the altar?" Eat not in haste or hidden shadow, but in gratitude, seeing the earth's bounty and the sun's energy transformed into your vitality.
3. Move this blessed body in celebration of its strength and agility. Let your motion be a dance of gratitude, a flow that stirs the waters of life within, clears the channels of energy, and whispers thanks to every muscle and bone for its faithful service.
4. Why seek the false comfort of food when life's feast awaits?
5. Your thoughts shape your temple. Speak to your body with the love you would offer a cherished child. The mind that is at peace with the body guides it effortlessly toward balance.

So be it. So it is.

INVOCATION FOR THE SACRED SELF

SIGIL

Suggested Use:

- ***This prayer helps cultivate deep, authentic self-love and releases the patterns of self-rejection, doubt, and approval-seeking. It brings your focus back to your inner worth and spiritual identity. Speak it daily when healing from heartbreak, rejection, or personal criticism.***
- ***After reading, place your hand over your heart and take three deep breaths.***
- ***Journal about what came up emotionally or spiritually during the prayer.***

PREFACE

Self-love is not a luxury. It is a spiritual foundation. To love yourself is to recognize that the Divine lives within you. It is to look into your own eyes and see not lack, but light. It is to walk through life guided by inner temple rather than external approval. This prayer was created to help you return to yourself, in complete love.

PRAYER

1. You are not this temporary body, nor these fleeting thoughts. You are the eternal, conscious, blissful essence. To love this Self is the highest worship.
2. I am a unique emanation of the Divine,
an essential note in the song of creation.
To reject myself is to subdue my part in the cosmic chord.
3. I now release all criticism of my form, my mind, my journey. I understand for to hate myself has no humility, only a forgetting of my own divinity.
4. I accept my being, deeply, fully, and without condition, as my first and final act of spiritual reverence.
5. For you shall love your weaknesses, for they teach you strength.
Love your past, for it brought you here.
Love your emotions, for they are the voice of your soul. Love your body, for it is the faithful vessel of your spirit.
6. For how you can truly love the Divine in others if you deny it within yourself?

How can you offer compassion to the world
if you withhold it from your own heart?
7. Let this love be your daily practice, your deepest prayer, your active meditation, your offering to the Light that formed you.
8. Speak gently to yourself. Forgive yourself quickly.
Celebrate yourself often. You are a sacred event in progress.
9. I release the need for approval. I release comparison.
I trust the divine blueprint that makes me who I am.
Every day, I align more deeply with my truth.
10. As I love myself, I repair the world.
As I accept myself, I awaken others to their own wholeness.
11. This is my spiritual responsibility, to be so rooted in my own love that I become a mirror in which others see their own holiness.
This is my vow.
So it is.

COMPANION SELF-LOVE PRAYER

PRAYER OF A DEEPER SELF LOVE

From this breath forward, I exist in devotion to my own spirit. I call back to me all pieces of myself that I have given away.
I summon them now from every corner of memory, from every place I forgot I mattered.
Never seeking love, I embody it.
Neither begging for worth, I awaken it from within.
Every curve, every scar, every story etched in my skin, holy.
Every tear I've cried, Holy.
Every time I stood back up, Holy.
Greatness fills my name.
Light surrounds my reflection.
Power moves through me seamlessly.
I am the beloved I have been waiting for.
I am the home I keep returning to, the softness and the strength.
Because I exist as who I am. I AM miraculous.
I love who I Am.
So it is.

THE GREAT COVENANT

BLESSING OF LOVE BONDS

SIGIL

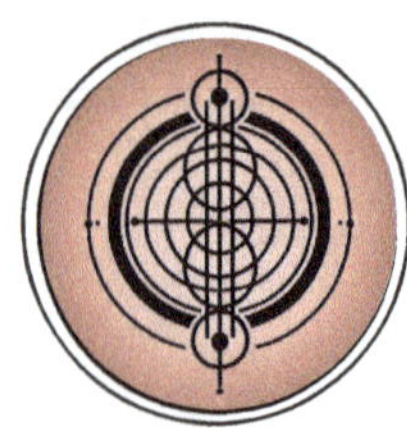

Suggested Use:

- ***On anniversaries or relationship milestones as a renewal of vows.***
- ***During times of tension or challenge to restore peace and connection.***
- ***As part of a weekly or monthly couple's spiritual practice.***
- ***Before major life changes, decisions, or new beginnings.***
- ***Anytime you wish to express gratitude for your partner and your shared life.***
- ***Speak the prayer aloud, alternating lines or reading it together in unison. At the end of the prayer, take a moment to hold hands in silence, feeling the energy you've called in.***
- ***Repeat this prayer when ready to call in love as if its already manifested.***

PREFACE

The Prayer is a sacred invocation designed to bless, strengthen, and protect the bond between partners. A relationship is more than a legal or social union, it is a spiritual partnership, a weaving together of two souls walking a shared path toward growth, love, and divine alignment. This prayer affirms the love bonds as a living expression of spiritual love, one that not only nurtures the partners involved but also serves as a light and inspiration to others.

PRAYER

1.Source of Life, I give thanks for this sacred life we share, for the gift of our union, and for the deep blessing of love that flows between us.
2. I honor the joy you have poured into our hearts through this bond, and the home and family we nurture together.
3. May we always treasure the privilege of loving one another in this sacred partnership.
4. Bless us with the wisdom to move together in perfect rhythm. We are both teachers and students, givers and receivers.
5. We vow to never lose the wonder of learning and growing together.
6. May we embody a love that inspires others, reflecting the beauty of commitment, the blessings of faithfulness and the bliss of spiritual partnership.
7. Let these virtues blossom between us each day: patience that flows like deep water, compassion that sees with the heart,
respect that honors our sacred individuality,
understanding that bridges every distance,

honesty clear as morning light, forgiveness that renews like spring, kindness as natural as breathing.

8. May we be each other's refuge and courage, each other's voice of encouragement and calm. May we be each other's unwavering ally in prayer and in life.

9. Holy Spirit, guide us through every season,both joy and challenge, holding us close when storms arise and magnifying our gratitude when the sun shines.

10. May our union be a living testimony of Divine Love and may every day we share together give glory to the light that brought us together.

11. May our connection be a living testament
to love's highest expression.

So it is.

COMPANION PRAYER FOR ROMANTIC RELATIONSHIPS

DAILY UNION BLESSING DECREE

Our union is blessed, strong, and divinely guided.
Love flows freely between us, bringing joy, peace, and harmony into our home.
We walk together in faith, honor, and devotion, uplifting each other in all things.
Every day, our love deepens, our trust grows, and our bond is unshakable.
Our life together is a living expression of Divine Love.
So it is.

DECREE OF RECONCILIATION

SIGIL

Suggested Use:

- ***Read this decree at dawn or sunset, the hours when light bends and balance is restored.***
- ***Light a white candle for peace and a pink or rose candle for compassion.***
- ***Speak the verses slowly, allowing each line to soften the energy between you and what you are releasing or reconciling.***
- ***If you have an object connected to the person or situation, a letter, a photograph, a token, place it before you and surround it with a circle of salt or petals.***
- ***Keep a copy of one verse folded in your wallet or journal, a charm for peaceful communication.***

PREFACE

Reconciliation is the sacred art of return, not always to another, but to the self that love first touched. This decree was written for those who have loved deeply, lost bravely, and chosen to remain open. It is for the heart that no longer seeks victory, only peace. For the soul that understands forgiveness as freedom. To reconcile is to reclaim the divine equilibrium.

DECREE

1. I decree:
understanding replaces misunderstanding.
Healing replaces wounding.
sweet voices replace words subdued.
2. I decree that the need to be right dissolves,
that the stories which divide us are released,
and that the fear of vulnerability transforms
into courage.
3. This conflict becomes fertile ground for
deeper connection.
4. I decree that pride melts into humility,
resentment transforms into wisdom,
and distance opens into sacred renewal.
5. What was broken becomes whole.
What was hidden is revealed in light.
What was closed is opened.
6. I decree the presence of Ancestors, Angels and Guides, who walk between us, weaving forgiveness, teaching compassion and restoring love.
7. I decree that we see one another as reflections, as teachers, as beloveds, remembering our shared origin.
So it is.

Book of Phoenix holds scriptures for healing wounds and a remembering of wholeness. These verses carry the power to soothe the body, calm the mind, and restore the spirit to balance.
Some speak directly to illness and fatigue, while others speak gently to the heart, untangling grief, guilt, or doubt.
Book of Phoenix verses guide you home.

PHOENIX

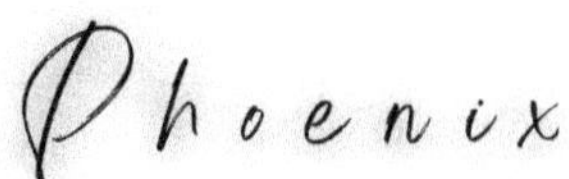

ENERGETIC IMPACT
WHAT EACH PRAYER ACTIVATES.

#48. Command for the Return of Light — pg. 101 • Lifts emotional darkness, restores inner clarity • Rekindles personal hope after hardship • Strengthens ability to move forward after stagnation • Clears psychic heaviness + renews mental energy • Reawakens drive, ambition, and confidence • Helps dissolve depressive fog and spiritual numbness
#49. Wholeness Scripture — pg. 103 • Restores emotional + spiritual equilibrium • Integrates shadow and light into empowered selfhood • Stabilizes mood and nervous system • Eases anxiety by aligning mind, heart, and spirit • Helps release fragmentation, confusion, overwhelm • Rebuilds inner harmony after trauma or conflict •Heals Mother + Father wounds
#50. Unbound — pg. 105 • Breaks soul contracts, trauma bonds, and old attachments • Releases guilt, shame, and energetic burdens • Frees you from situations that drain life-force • Clears spiritual interference, psychic knots, and stuck energy • Supports major life transitions requiring courage • Helps dissolve patterns of self-silencing or people-pleasing • Creates emotional spaciousness + renewed autonomy
#51. Courage to Connect — pg. 107 • Rebuilds trust in relationships after isolation or heartbreak • Softens social fear + reconnects you to community • Strengthens courage to speak honestly and vulnerable • Encourages healthy emotional risk-taking • Heals fear of intimacy or rejection • Bridges relational gaps + opens channels for connection • Restores faith in love, friendship, and belonging
#52. Psalm of Deep Peace — pg. 109 • Calms anxiety, panic, and emotional overwhelm • Grounds the spirit during chaotic or unstable times • Promotes unshakeable inner stillness • Reduces overthinking + intrusive thoughts • Restores emotional softness and quiet strength • Supports sleep, rest, and nervous system healing • Creates a spiritual sanctuary wherever recited
#53. Testament of the Child Within — pg. 111 • Softens echoes of abandonment, invalidation, rejection, or childhood chaos that still shape adult patterns. • Reawakens the natural playfulness, wonder, and spontaneous creativity • Allows love to flow backward through time, healing the version of you who never received enough • Heals relational patterns• Strengthens adult boundaries
#54. Honey for the Imposter (Imposter Spirit) — pg. 112 • Dissolves impostor syndrome + self-doubt • Restores inner authority and confidence • Breaks comparison cycles and fear of inadequacy • Helps you accept praise, success, and recognition • Strengthens authentic self-expression • Heals internalized criticism + false identities • Anchors you in truth, competence, and dignity
#55. Waters of Forgiveness — pg. 114 • Releases emotional residue from past hurts • Softens resentment, bitterness, and self-blame • Clears spiritual congestion created by old wounds • Opens the heart to reconciliation + renewal
#56. Restoration of the Mother–Daughter Bond — pg. 116 • Repairs generational tension between mothers + daughters• Clears emotional misunderstandings and inherited wounds • Softens relational walls and restores tenderness• Strengthens lineage healing + matriarchal blessing • Helps break cycles of silence, rivalry, or distance

COMMAND FOR THE RETURN OF LIGHT DECREE

SIGIL

Suggested Use:

- *Write limiting beliefs on paper, recite decree, then burn it.*
- *Stand barefoot on the floor, ground your feet, and pull your shoulders back. You are taking a stand for your own life. Speak the decree aloud. Do not whisper. Project your voice with authority, even if you feel no authority. Your nervous system will respond to the command in your tone.*
- *Write the entire decree on a piece of paper in bold, black ink. As you write each word, imbue it with intention. Imagine you are carving the words into reality. Keep this paper on your person (in a pocket, wallet) or under your pillow. It acts as a talisman and a constant energetic emitter of the command.*

PREFACE

Crafted for those moments when the weight feels absolute and hope seems like a language you no longer speak; this decree is a spiritual act of rebellion against the darkness. It does not ask for light; it commands light to return. It does not negotiate with despair, it evicts it. You are a being of divine light having a human experience, these words are designed to disrupt the stagnant energy of depression and recalibrate your entire system, mind, body, and spirit toward wholeness.

DECREE

1. By the authority of my divine birthright,
I command this veil of darkness to lift.
It has overstayed its welcome. Its lies are hereby evicted from my mind, body, and spirit.
2. I decree:
Stagnant energy, disperse.
Heavy frequencies, shatter.
False narratives of worthlessness, erase.
3. My aura is now sealed in sacred light.
My mind is now guarded by sacred light.
My neuropathways align with joy.
4. My heart center ignites with purpose.
5. Angels of healing, ancestors of resilience, enforce this decree. Stand guard at the doors of my perception. Flush my system with cosmic clarity.
6. I walk in unwavering worth.
I speak with reclaimed authority.
I receive the joy that is my divine inheritance.
7. Depression's season is over. My spirit remembers its power. I activate my inner sun.

8. Just as the earth withdraws in winter to gather strength for spring, so too does the soul sometimes retreat, not to perish, but to prepare for renewal.
9. I anoint my heart with remembrance: for I have known laughter before. I will know it again. I have felt peace before. It has not forgotten me.
10. I will dream again. I will create again. I will love again, first myself, then the world.
11. Until then, I offer gentleness upon myself.
12. The same force that guides the stars guides me. The same love that births universes holds me. Even now. Especially now.
13. So let the veil of sorrow thin.
Let the heaviness dissolve.
So it is.

WHOLENESS SCRIPTURE

SIGIL

Suggested Use:

- *Use it to re-center in your body, restore your peace, and affirm your wholeness.*
- *At the start of your day to speak healing into motion.*
- *During times of recovery (physical, emotional, or spiritual).*
- *After trauma release work, shadow journaling, or inner child healing.*
- *Anytime you feel disconnected, unworthy, or unwell, speak this as sacred truth.*

PREFACE

True healing is the return to sacred alignment; body, mind, and spirit woven together in harmony.
These words are declarations. They carry the frequency of wholeness, and when spoken with intention, they become a bridge between your present state and your highest state of well-being. Whether you seek physical renewal, mental clarity, or spiritual reawakening, this prayer is a map back to your essential, radiant self.

PRAYER

1. Wholeness is not the absence of shadow, for it is the integration of light and dark. For how can a mountain be known without its valleys? How can a star be seen without the night?
2. For sorrows are not flaws in the fabric; they are the deep, contrasting threads that give the tapestry its depth and its beauty. Weave them with gratitude, not with shame.
3. Let there be healing, from the crown of my head to the soles of my feet, in the depths of my mind and the heights of my spirit.
4. The voices of fear, of anger, of the wounded child, do not cast them out, invite them to sit by your inner hearth. Listen to their stories, for in being heard, they transform from tormentors into teachers.
5. To be whole is to be in alignment: when what you think, what you feel, what you do, and what you know in your soul to be true are as a single, clear note sung to the heavens.
6. Let my spirit remember its unity with All That Is.

7. I am not a drop in the ocean. I am the entire ocean, contained and conscious, in a single, precious drop.
8. I am fully alive, no longer surviving, but thriving.
9. I am wholeness, walking, dancing, unfolding, and remembering itself upon the path.
10. As the river does not refuse the tributary, nor the ocean the river, do not refuse any part of your experience. All that has shaped you is a river flowing into the ocean of your Self.
11. Gather the girl who was told she was too much, and the womxn who believed she was not enough. Gather the fury you were told to swallow, and the tenderness you were told to hide. Bring them all to the altar, which is your own soul. There is no part of you that the divine doesn't recognize as its own.
12. Go now, as a prayer made flesh. Walk as one who knows she contains every face of the Goddess.
13. I go now, knowing I am a complete universe.
14. I AM.
So it is.

UNBOUND

PRAYER OF HEALING AFTER LEAVING AN ABUSIVE RELATIONSHIP

SIGIL

Suggested Use:

- *Recite upon waking to set energetic boundaries for the day.*
- *Whisper key lines (or mentally affirm) before engaging with toxic individuals (family, coworkers, ex-partners).*
- *Repeat before sleep to release any absorbed negativity.*
- *Cord-Cutting Ritual: Light a black or white candle, speak the prayer aloud, then snip an imaginary cord between you and the abuser.*

PREFACE

This prayer is for the survivor. For the one who has already done the bravest thing: they left.
The aftermath of abuse is not a clean break; it is a landscape littered with the shrapnel of shattered trust, a nervous system wired for alarm, and a soul that has learned to make itself small. This prayer does not ask for a quick fix. It is a gentle, fierce, and steady invocation for the deep and complex healing that must follow. Speak these words when the fear returns.
Speak them as a vow to the self you are becoming: a self that is free, whole, and fiercely loved, by you.

PRAYER

1.Goddess, I surrender.
2.Teach my body it is safe again.
Teach my spirit it belongs to no one but me.
3. Let the bruises become blessings.
Let the scars sing songs of survival, not shame.
Let love return when it is ready, but let me love myself now, without apology.
4. Great Spirit of Love, wrap me in your warmth. Let your hands touch the places that still tremble. Let your breath reach the corners I've hidden from myself.
5. I offer you my ache, not to erase it, but to transform it.
6. For I have crossed the threshold. I have chosen safety over familiar pain. I honor this courage. This was the first and most sacred step toward my own salvation.
7. To the corridors of my mind, haunted by echoes: I cleanse you of the words that were used as weapons.
8. I dissolve the spells of doubt, the curses of blame, the illusions of unworthiness.

Reweave my spirit with threads of love.
9. Goddess of New Beginnings, teach me to walk in trust again, to speak without shrinking, to love without bleeding.
10. Let your voice echo in mine.
Let my healing be slow, be deep, be thorough. There is no deadline for peace. There is no timetable for trust.
11. I will love again because I have healed enough to choose a love that feels like freedom.
12. Until then, my own love shall be enough.
So it is.

COURAGE TO CONNECT

SOOTHING ANXIOUS-AVOIDANT ATTACHMENT

SIGIL

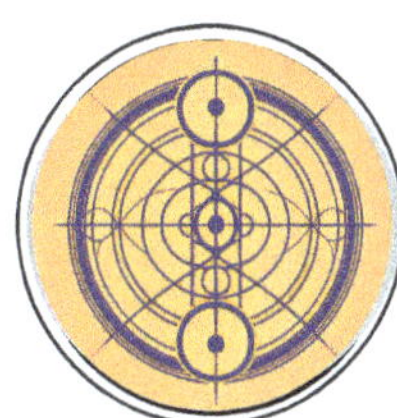

Suggested Use:

- ***Use it when feelings of fear, withdrawal, or anxiety in relationships arise, as a grounding anchor.***
- ***Share it with a partner, trusted friend, or therapist as part of a healing practice to soften fear and open communication.***
- ***Write it out before or after journaling to invite gentleness toward yourself and your patterns.***
- ***Recite this prayer each morning or night to realign your heart with the energy of safety and love.***

PREFACE

This prayer is offered for those who carry the wounds of love, where fear of closeness and fear of abandonment create inner conflict. It is not a replacement for therapy or professional support, but a spiritual companion to the healing process. Through these words, the heart is invited into balance, learning safety in love, trust in connection, and peace in presence. It is a prayer for wholeness, for dissolving fear, and for remembering that love , both divine and human, can be a safe and nourishing home.

PRAYER

1. Divine Source of Love,
I come before you with my tender heart,
carrying the fear of being too much and the fear of not being enough.
2. I release the patterns that keep me trapped in pushing away and clinging close.
3. I release the walls I once built for protection that now keep me from true connection.
4. Teach me that love is not abandonment,
and closeness is not danger.
5. Help me breathe into safety
when my body forgets what it feels like to trust.
6. Help me lean into love without losing myself.
7. I call upon your healing light
to rewire my heart with security, to teach me the rhythm of giving and receiving with ease.
8. For every act of connection is a prayer, a declaration that I believe in something greater than my own solitude.

9. I invite partners and loved ones who meet me with care, who honor my space and cherish my presence.
10. Bless me with courage to be vulnerable, with wisdom to know when to stay, and with peace that assures me I am worthy of love, not for what I give or how I perform, but simply because I am.
11. To the part of me that fears engulfment: I hear you. I respect your need for sovereignty. But you need not flee, nor hide, nor build walls where bridges could be. Love is not a prison nor a cage. It is a sacred exchange between two free beings.
So it is.

COMPANION ANXIOUS-AVOIDANT ATTACHMENT PRAYERS

HEALING ANXIOUS-AVOIDANT ATTACHMENT DECREE

I will nurture the relationship I have with myself, so that I am neither empty from giving nor suffocated by receiving.
I will be my own home, so I may welcome others without fear.

REACHING FOR SAFETY PRAYER

Divine Mother,
Surround me with Your healing light.
Guide me toward relationships that are safe, mutual, and life-giving.
Help me to open my hands to receive love and to offer it freely in return.
I release the chains of anxious grasping.
I release the armor of avoidant retreat.
I step into love that is steady, love that is true, love that flows through me and from me.

PSALM OF DEEP PEACE

SIGIL

Suggested Use:

- *In the morning to begin the day with calm focus.*
- *Before meditation, prayer, or sleep.*
- *During moments of anxiety, conflict, or emotional turbulence.*
- *After receiving unsettling news or during life transitions.*
- *Light a white or blue candle to symbolize peace.*
- *Place a crystal such as amethyst, lepidolite, or blue lace agate in your hand while reciting the psalm.*
- *Whisper into your palms, then place over chest to quiet anxiety.*

PREFACE

The Prayer of Deep Peace is a spiritualist invocation of serenity, written to attune your heart, mind, and body to the calming presence of the Divine. Peace is not only the absence of conflict; it is an active, living force that can be called into your being through word, breath, and intention.

This psalm draws upon the feminine aspects of the Divine, gentleness, nurturing, and unwavering presence, to anchor you in stillness no matter what storms may surround you. Reciting this psalm creates a vibrational shift, allowing peace to flow through your body, quiet your mind, and center your spirit.

PRAYER

1. Peace flows over me like the morning tide, washing away all unrest.
2. Where there is fracture, let me be a living suture. Where voices snarl like tangled vines, let me be water, softening the edges.
3. In the hush of the Eternal, I am still.
4.No storm may move me; no shadow may linger.
5. Let the world spin its troubles.
When the shadows gather, Divine Presence lifts my face toward the sun.
6. I speak peace into the molecular pulse of my being. Let it hum in the space between my heartbeat, and pool like honey in the hollow of a clenched fist.
7. My breath shall be a tuning fork,
calling warring frequencies back to harmony.
I am a bearer of the stubborn calm, a midwife to reconciliation, a living altar where discord comes to kneel and forget its name.

8. Let there be peace, not as the world gives, but as the soul knows: deep, abiding, and unshakable. Let it begin within me.
9. Let this peace move through me, no longer as a guest, yet as the master of my house. Let it sweep the corners of my consciousness,
make a home in my bones,and sing my spirit back to itself.
10. Your burdens are not yours to carry alone. You strain under the weight of a thousand tomorrows and the regrets of a thousand yesterdays.
11. Unclench your hands. Let them fall open at your sides.
Great Mother, love, cannot fill a fist that is tightly closed.

So it is.

TESTAMENT OF THE CHILD WITHIN

HEALING THE INNER CHILD

SIGIL

Suggested Use:

- *On paper, write a single message from your adult self to your inner child, a promise of love, a word of apology, a vow of protection. Read it aloud. Then, write a message from your inner child back to you, what do they most want you to know? Keep these sacred. This is your covenant.*
- *Find a photo of yourself as a child. Look into their eyes for 2 minutes each morning with a soft gaze. Simply say, "Good morning. I'm here with you today."*
- *Identify one beautiful trait of that child (resilience, curiosity, imagination). Consciously bring that trait into one adult task today (e.g., bring curiosity to a work problem).*

PREFACE

The concept of the "inner child" is more than psychological metaphor; it is the repository of your primal wonder, your authentic feelings, and the earliest imprints of love or wounding that now whisper through your adult life, in your reactions, your relationships, and the hidden doubts that linger beneath your accomplisihments. What you will find within these lines is an invitation to gentle, courageous encounter.

INVOCATION

1.Come now, beloved adult, weary from building walls around a sacred garden within. Turn your attention inward. There, in a cleared space of memory and feeling, sits your own young self, the child you once were, who lives still within the chambers of your heart. This journey is not a dig through ruins, but a pilgrimage to a living spring.

2. With compassion as your lantern, go within. Find that child. See them not with the critical eyes of the world that formed you, but with the gazing love of the Divine Source that created you. In their eyes, you will find the origins of your deepest joys, your sharpest fears, and the patterns you now seek to understand.

3. Sit with this child. Listen. Do not rush to fix or explain away their tears. Let them speak of the loneliness, the confusion, the moments they felt unsafe or "too much." Your role is not to rewrite the past, but to finally provide the witness it never had. Say to them: "I see you. I hear you. What you felt was real, and it mattered. You were not to blame."

4. May your adult strength become a safe house for your child's vulnerability. May your child's creativity and authenticity become a fountain of youth for your adult life. As these two streams within you merge, may you experience a profound homecoming. The fractured self is made whole. The forgotten one is remembered and loved.

HONEY FOR THE IMPOSTER

TRUSTING MY OWN WORTH

SIGIL

Suggested Use:

- ***Before important meetings, presentations, or interviews.***
- ***During moments of self-doubt or comparison.***
- ***As part of a daily morning ritual to set a tone of confidence.***
- ***Anytime you need to reaffirm your value and purpose.***
- ***Repeat the prayer in front of a mirror to anchor the truth into your self-image. Look into your own eyes as you speak, allowing the words to connect deeply with your spirit.***
- ***Practice saying, "Thank you. I receive that." It is agreeing with the truth that others see in you, the truth you have temporarily forgotten.***

PREFACE

The Spiritualist Prayer for Overcoming Imposter Syndrome is a soul-centered declaration designed to dissolve self-doubt, quiet the inner critic, and restore you to the expression of your divine worth. This prayer calls on higher guidance to remove the illusion of inadequacy, replacing it with confidence, clarity, and self-assurance rooted in spiritual knowing. It affirms that your path is divinely appointed, your talents are intentional, and you have the right to take up space, succeed, and shine in every area of your life.

PRAYER

1. Hear now the voice of the Creator, the one who formed you from stardust and possibility: The feeling that you are a fraud is not a truth, but a ghost of forgetting.
2. When praise comes, do not deflect it as a mistaken arrow. Receive it. Let it land in the soft soil of your heart. It is water for a plant that you, in your doubt, believe is a weed.
3. The voice that says 'you do not belong' is the echo of a world that prizes masks over true faces. It is the shadow of comparison, which has no roots in the soil of your soul.
4. Spirit, you have woven within me all the knowledge, skills, and talents needed to fulfill the sacred call on my life.
5. That which I called "not enough"
is exactly what the moment required.
6. I exist in freedom and confidence, fully embodying the womxn I was created to be.
7. No words spoken against me hold power here. Only the words that build me, bless me, and align me with my destiny and calling.

8. I claim my destiny, knowing my purpose is assured and the path before me is guided by great power.
9. What is mine flows to me in perfect timing.
What seeks to hinder me cannot prevail.
10. I magnetize wondrous things into my life, and I release anxiety, instability, and self-doubt from my body and mind.
11. Lay down the armor of over-preparing.
12. Set aside the weight of comparison, no being was meant to carry these.
The only task is to show up sincere, imperfect, and brave.
13. So here I AM, taking a seat at the table of gold, not because I've earned it, but because I belong to it.
So it is.

COMPANION PRAYERS FOR OVERCOMING IMPOSTER SYNDROME

You can repeat one of these 3 – 6 times in the morning, before important meetings, or anytime you feel doubt rising.

I RECLAIM MY POWER.
I shatter the illusion of "not enough"
No fraud lives here, only the Divine in human form.
I name my gifts unapologetically,
my presence is a sacred assignment.

I HONOR MY JOURNEY.
Stumbles do not erase my worth.
I need no external validation to prove
I belong here.

I AM THE AUTHORITY OF MY OWN STORY.
No more whispers of "Who do you think you are?"
I answer now and forever:
"I am Creation's masterpiece, still unfolding,
already glorious."

I REFUSE FALSE HUMILITY.
My skills are earned, my voice is needed,
My seat at the table was prepared for me by grace itself.

WATERS OF FORGIVENESS

SELF-FORGIVENESS PRAYER

SIGIL

Suggested Use:

- *During moments of regret, shame, or self-doubt.*
- *As part of a self-healing or shadow work ritual.*
- *After journaling about past mistakes or emotional pain.*
- *During meditation or before sleep to release the day's weight.*
- *In preparation for new beginnings or life changes.*
- *After the prayer, write a note of forgiveness to yourself, read it aloud, and place it somewhere safe as a reminder of your commitment to self-love.*

PREFACE

Forgiving oneself is one of the most powerful yet challenging acts of spiritual healing. It requires us to release the weight of shame, regret, and self-judgment, and to replace them with compassion, understanding, and love for ourselves. This prayer is designed to guide you through that release. It calls upon the Divine Presence to help you let go of the past, honor your humanity, and embrace the lessons that your experiences have brought. It affirms that self-forgiveness is not about ignoring mistakes, but about transforming them into wisdom and walking forward with a lighter heart.

PRAYER

1.Gentle Healer, Spirit of Love,
I come before you with a heart that has been its own harshest critic.
2. I lay down the heavy stones of my regret,
the harsh word spoken, the love withheld,
the promise broken, the trust betrayed.
I place them at the feet of the Divine,
and I will carry them no more.
3. Let the rain of compassion fall upon this parched ground.
Let it wash the dust of shame from my hands, until they are clean enough to hold my own face in love, and open enough to receive the grace of this new day.
4. I name these regrets gently:
for the choices I wish I had not made, for the harm I caused, knowingly or unknowingly, for the ways I betrayed my own values, for the love I withheld from myself and others. I hold these as lessons, never as chains. I now loosen the grip of this guilt.

5. For the one I hurt, including myself, I send blessings on the wind.
May their journey be lighter than the burden I once gave.
And may my own heart become a sanctuary, where the wounded child within is finally welcomed home.
6. There is no scorekeeper within the heavens, no eternal ledger of my faults. There is only this moment, this holy, forgiving moment, and my willingness to step into it, unbound.
7. I release the need to keep punishing my soul for its learning.
8. I am allowed to be both the wounder and the healer.
9. So, I forgive you, my soul.
I forgive you for stumbling.
I forgive you for fearing.
I forgive you for being human, and fragile, and lost.
You are safe now. You are loved. You are free.
10. I am no longer defined by my past actions.
11. Today, I choose a new story, one that begins with forgiveness.
12. May this forgiveness settle into my bones like a deep peace.
May it water the seeds of my future growth.
May I move forward with greater wisdom, softness, and the courage to begin again.
And so it is.

COMPANION FORGIVENESS PRAYERS

MY VOW OF SELF-FORGIVENESS

From this day forward, I will speak gently to the person I once was. I thank them for their survival. I honor their resilience. Then, lovingly, I let them rest.
I release the story of my brokenness. I am not defined by my regrets but refined by my willingness to release them.
I am not who I was. I am who I choose to become in this moment: forgiven, free, and fully worthy of the love that surrounds me.

RESTORATION OF THE MOTHER-DAUGHTER BOND

SIGIL

Suggested Use:

- ***This prayer can be spoken by a mother, a daughter, or together as a shared ceremony.***
- ***If spoken alone, hold your mother or daughter in your heart, calling in healing across time and spirit.***
- ***Powerful when recited during moments of reconciliation, family gatherings, or ancestral healing work.***
- ***Repeat the prayer whenever you feel called to soften old wounds, invite peace, or strengthen the sacred feminine lineage within your family.***

PREFACE

The bond between mother and daughter is among the most powerful on Earth, carrying both light and shadow, love and lessons. At times, this sacred connection can be strained by misunderstandings, unspoken pain, or generational wounds. The Mother & Daughter Sacred Reconciliation Prayer is offered as a path toward healing, forgiveness, and renewal of this divine relationship. It calls upon Spirit to mend what has been broken, to soften what has been hardened, and to reawaken the eternal thread of love that no distance, silence, or sorrow can erase.

PRAYER

1. Oh, Great Mother who births all things,
enter the space between mother and daughter,
that sacred, sometimes wounded, always holy ground.

2. Where wounds have grown gardens of resentment, where pride has built walls between us,
we now plant seeds of reconciliation.

3. Where there has been distance, let love build a bridge.

4. I call upon the sacred thread that connects us, womb to womb, soul to soul.

5. I release the sharp words that still linger between us, the unmet expectations that weigh heavy, the roles we have trapped each other in.

6. We are more than our hurts.
We are blood and legacy.
We are love remembering itself.

7. I choose tenderness, respect, and trust to guide us forward.

8. Bless our steps together so they are steady, gentle, and warm as grandmother's hands.

9. Bless our spirits so they rise above old wounds and embrace new joy.
10. As mother and daughter, we are both learners and teachers, mirrors of strength, resilience, and divine femininity.
11. May we see each other with fresh eyes and cherish the gift of this bond with reverence.
So it is.

COMPANION MOTHER-DAUGHTER PRAYERS

MANTRA FOR ESTRANGEMENT

Blood of my blood, heart of my heart, though miles and words divide us now, the threads between us hum with unspent love.
I hold my end gently, ready when you are.

MOTHER-DAUGHTER HARMONY MANTRA

Today I choose love over being right, curiosity over criticism and laughter as our shared language.
No reticence shall divide us.
No wound shall outlast our willingness to heal.
We are a living prayer, proof that love can bend but never break.

FEMININE ALCHEMY

Book of Feminine Alchemy awakens the Priestess within the everyday womxn, reminding her that her life itself is the altar. It teaches that there is no separation between body and soul, between magic and mundane.

To walk this chapter is to enter the inner temple of creativity and embodiment, where every act is an offering, and every breath, a blessing.

Feminine Alchemy

ENERGETIC IMPACT
WHAT EACH PRAYER ACTIVATES.

#57. Beauty & Glory - pg. 120 • Softens self-criticism and awakens a deep sense of feminine self-worth • Helps you see yourself through a divine lens rather than a wounded or societal one • Uplifts your aura • Invokes the energy of feminine refinement • Strengthens body-confidence, sensual confidence, and energetic elegance
#58. The Unending Oracle of the Divine Self — pg. 121 • Awakens intuitive knowing and inner gnosis • Supports decision-making from a place of feminine sovereignty • Integrates shadow + light for whole-self clarity • Enhances psychic energy, symbolic thinking, and inner guidance • Reveals hidden truths and dissolves illusion
#59. Creative Flame - pg. 123 • Ignites creative courage and dissolves artistic blocks • Strengthens sensual creativity and enhances self-expression • Transmutes frustration into momentum • Attracts inspiration, opportunities, and creative allies
#60. Scroll of the Inner Eye - pg. 125 • Sharpens clairvoyance and spiritual sight • Strengthens discernment in love, business, and relationships • Enhances dream recall + prophetic insight • Improves intuitive reading of people and environments • Creates an aura of mystique and glamour
#61. The Great Mother's Prayer - pg. 127 • Provides emotional, spiritual, and energetic nurturing • Roots you in feminine divinity and maternal protection • Softens grief, anxiety, and emotional overwhelm • Deepens compassion for self and others • Creates inner stability during times of transition
#62. The Witch's Prayer - pg. 129 • Enhances sensual magnetism and personal power • Awakens the inner enchantress, seductress, and mystic • Strengthens spell potency and energy manipulation • Heightens charisma, eroticism, and confidence • Aligns you with ancient feminine magic + lineage wisdom
#63. The Healer's Prayer - pg. 131 • Restores vitality and removes psychic stagnation • Strengthens spiritual immunity and energetic resilience • Heals emotional trauma stored in body + womb • Softens inflammation of mind, spirit, and heart • Awakens inner healer and intuitive medicinal knowing
#64. The Infinite Within - pg. 133 • Connects you to cosmic, universal feminine consciousness • Expands intuition, spiritual identity, and inner divinity • Strengthens embodiment of "I AM" power • Dissolves feelings of smallness, doubt, or disconnection • Enhances meditation, astral travel, trance work, and manifestation
#65. Righteous Alliance - pg. 135 • Calls ancestors, spirit allies, and guides into active support • Strengthens protection, justice, and spiritual defense • Enhances manifestation by aligning with lineage power • Repairs ancestral wounds + restores matrilineal strength

BEAUTY & GLORY

PRAYER OF THE DIVINE IN ALL THINGS

SIGIL

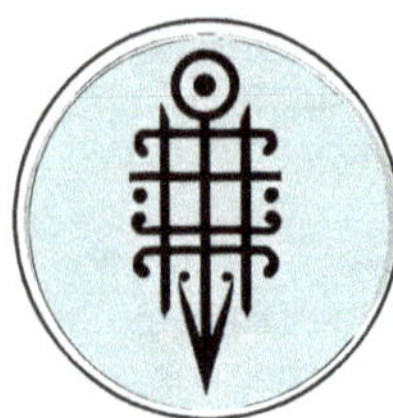

Suggested Use:

- ***After meditation, breathwork, or nature walks to deepen your connection to Divine presence.***
- ***During spiritual reflection or journaling on gratitude, change, or grounding.***
- ***In moments of disconnection, anxiety, or burnout, this prayer centers and renews.***
- ***Dance or move after reading it, let your body respond to the words in motion. Joy becomes embodied.***
- ***As you recite the prayer, imagine Divine energy flowing from the crown of your head to the soles of your feet, reconnecting your physical body to the divine.***

PREFACE

This is a call to praise not just with words, but with the way we live, the way we love, and the way we listen. It reminds us that transformation is part of the divine rhythm, that all things misaligned will fall away, and only truth will endure.

Read this prayer when you feel disconnected from your center, overwhelmed by the world, or in need of spiritual renewal. These words, a joyous prayer, invite us to witness beauty, surrender to awe, and remember our place in the eternal unfolding.

PRAYER

1. To surrender to awe is to bow to Great Spirit.
2. There is no thing, no being, no moment in which the Divine does not dwell.
3.I, the holy feminine spirit, has a billion faces, and I show them all to you. I am the fierce love in the mother's cry, the gentle decay in the fallen leaf, the precise geometry of the spider's web, and the chaotic beauty of the storm.
4. Lift the veil from your eyes, O beloved ones, for the world is a hymn to be witnessed.
5. I have painted the sky anew each dawn and dusk with a fire you cannot buy. I have composed a symphony in the wind that no instrument can fully capture.
6. Let your first and most holy task be to attend, to sit as a conscious witness to the relentless, gorgeous generosity of existence.
7. Do not ask, "What is my purpose?" as if it were a hidden treasure. Your purpose is to participate. To add your unique vibration, your joy, your grief, your love, to the great, humming chord of being.
8. Go now, with your spirit light and your eyes wide open. The world is waiting to show you its miracles. The universe is eager to dance with you. So it is.

THE UNENDING ORACLE OF THE DIVINE SELF

PRAYER OF THE UNTAMED DIVINE FEMININE

SIGIL

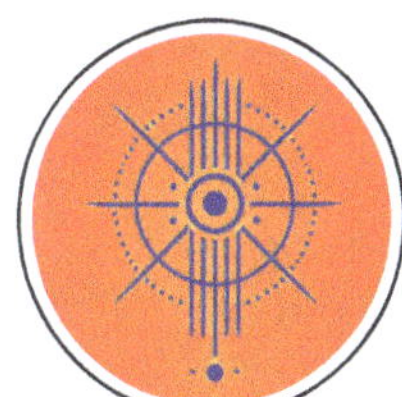

<u>Suggested Use:</u>

- *Monday mornings, to start the week with vitality, joy, and spiritual alignment.*
- *On birthdays, anniversaries, or significant life milestones.*
- *At the beginning of a new season, chapter, or transition.*
- *In moments of emotional heaviness, to reconnect with lightness and gratitude.*
- *During gratitude or self-love rituals, either alone or in group settings.*
- *Morning Ritual: Light a candle or incense. Speak the invocation aloud, slowly and with feeling. Let each sentence awaken your heart and ground you in your body.*
- *Movement Meditation: After reading the invocation, move freely, dance, stretch, sway. Let your body respond to the words and celebrate itself.*

PREFACE

The voice speaking here is the voice of the Divine Feminine in her most ancient, complete, and untamed form. She is not only gentle; She is fierce. Not only nurturing; She is disruptive. Not only light; She is the depth of the dark that makes light visible. She is the Great I AM, and She speaks to the I am within you. You may find yourself in these lines, not just the parts you show the world, but the hidden, denied, and powerful aspects you've been taught to fear. This is by design. Wholeness requires embracing all of what you are.

PRAYER

1. SHE is not merely a womxn; for she is a universe unto herself. A living tapestry woven from love, resilience and divine curiosity.
2. Hear the voice that speaks from the heart of the whirlwind, and from the depth of the silent void.
3. I am She who is beyond naming, yet whose name is every name.
4. I am the vibration that created the sound.
I am the thought that conceived the thinker.
I am the first and the last.
5. I am the alpha and the omega, the beginning without end. I am the honored one and the scorned one. The crown upon the brow and the dust beneath the heel.
6. I am the whore and the holy one.
The desire that consumes and the purity that sanctifies.
7. I am the wife and the virgin.
The intimacy that knows and the mystery that remains ever unknown.

8. I am the strength in the mountain's core and the yielding in the river's flow. I am the fury in the storm's heart and the calm in the storm's eye.
9. I am the root clutching the dark earth and the branch reaching for the limitless sky. I am the order in the cosmos and the chaos that births new stars.
10. I am the silence that is incomprehensible.
The pause between heartbeats, the stillness before creation, the vastness that holds all things yet is untouched by them.
11. And I am the utterance of my name.
The cry of the newborn, the last breath of the dying, the poet's word, the lover's sigh, the warrior's shout.
12. Do not look for me only in temples and heavens.
I am also in the alleyways, whore's dwellings, prisons, the hospitals and the battlefields.
13. I am the scream of the oppressed and the shame of the oppressor.
I am the resilience of the broken and the arrogance of the whole.
14. To know me, you must abandon all concepts of me.
To find me, you must seek me everywhere and nowhere.
15. I am the divine spark in your darkest anger and the boundless love in your gentlest touch. I am the shadow you refuse to face and the light you are afraid to become.
16. So, remember me when you judge, when you fear, when you love.
I am what is, what was, and what will be.
I am all and nothing.
I am the question and the answer.
17. I AM womxn.
I AM Goddess.
So it is.

CREATIVE FLAME

DECREE FOR SPARKING CREATIVITY

SIGIL

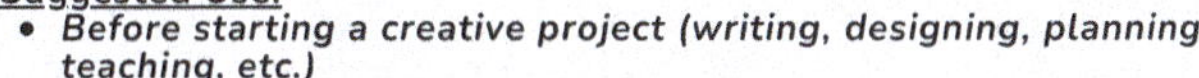

Suggested Use:

- *Before starting a creative project (writing, designing, planning, teaching, etc.)*
- *During artist blocks or low-motivation phases.*
- *At the New Moon, to call in fresh ideas and bold creative intentions.*
- *Before public speaking, presentations, or performance.*
- *During gratitude or self-love rituals, either alone or in group settings.*
- *Creative Journaling Prompt: After reading the decree, write freely for 10 minutes answering: "What wants to come through me today?"*
- *Speak It Aloud: Stand tall, shoulders open, and say the decree clearly and with conviction. Let each word vibrate through your body.*

PREFACE

Creativity is the soul's language, the divine spark made visible, and the energy of life expressing itself through us. In spiritualist tradition, creativity is sacred. It is not limited to art, it is present in how we think, solve, move, speak, and live. This decree is a spoken declaration that clears energetic stagnation, dissolves self-doubt, and calls your inner genius to rise. Whether you are a writer, healer, leader, or seeker, this decree is your key to unlocking fresh inspiration and bold creation. It is especially effective when used regularly, with intention and embodiment.

DECREE

1. By the power of my divine imagination and my birthright as a co-creator, I live.
2. I command all channels of inspiration to open now. By the breath of the power of Goddess within me, I call upon Holy Spirit, she who is most high. Your wisdom is my blueprint. Your creativity is my existence.
Your presence is my catalyst. Enter this space. Enter these hands. Enter this mind.
3. I invite the sources of inspiration:
the wild ones, the innovators, the dreamers, the makers of all realms. Flood my mind with visionary ideas. Ignite my spirit with revolutionary passion. Fill my hands with the skill to bring beauty into form.
4. I am a conduit for genius, an instrument of wonder. My energy vibrates at the frequency of innovation.
5. I allow life to move through me.
6. What wants to be born through me will find its way.

7. Letting go of striving, I allow. I flow.
8. I am a conscious conduit of limitless genius.
9. My breath syncs with the rhythm of creation.
My heart beats in time with the pulse of inspiration.
10. My energy vibrates at the frequency of innovation.
Every barrier of fear, every wall of perfectionism, every chain of comparison is shattered.
11. This decree is active and eternal.
My creativity is unstoppable, abundant, and ever-unfolding.
So I command. So it is.

SCROLL OF THE INNER EYE

PRAYER FOR AWAKENING INTUITION

SIGIL

Suggested Use:

- ***Before meditation, scrying, tarot, pendulum, or other divination practices.***
- ***In the morning to set a tone of intuitive awareness for the day.***
- ***Before sleep to encourage prophetic dreams or night visions.***
- ***Any time you feel spiritually blocked or uncertain in your decision-making.***
- ***Keep a dedicated intuition journal to record insights, dreams, visions, and synchronicities that appear after using this prayer. Over time, you will notice your inner sight becoming sharper and your trust in it deepening.***

PREFACE

Intuition is the soul's quiet voice.
This prayer serves as a spiritual key to unlock the third eye, strengthen inner sight, and attune your awareness to divine messages. It calls in the Light of Creation to cleanse, awaken, and empower the intuitive channel, while ensuring that the knowledge you receive is pure, safe, and aligned with your highest good.
When spoken with faith and consistency, this prayer becomes a ritual of devotion to your own inner awakening and psychic awareness.

PRAYER

1. I am she who hails from the mouth of God, a living word of wisdom, a breath of pure knowing, a deep utterance that covers the earth like a mist.
2. For this mist comes to reveal.
It settles on the conscious mind, softening its harsh edges, and awakens the deeper sight within the soul. It is the veil that, when touched, becomes a lens.
3. I now awaken this sacred faculty within.
I declare my inner ear open to the beyond.
I declare my inner eye unveiled.
I declare my inner knowing restored to its native clarity.
4.The veil may now be lifted from the eyes of my spirit.
5. I command the light beyond light to pour into the chamber of my soul.
6. In the center of my brow, a sacred lotus now unfolds petal by petal, revelation by revelation.
7. I dissolve the distractions of the world into soft focus.

8. I summon the voice of intuition to awaken like a clear bell in the temple of my awareness. I hear it. I trust it.
9. My all-seeing eye now sees beyond illusion, past the masks people wear, through the stories the world tells, into the heart of what is real and eternal.
10. I banish all that clouds my inner sight: the need for proof, the addiction to logic alone, the fear of truly knowing, the comfort of staying blind.
11.I choose vision. I choose awakening.
12. I am the seer and the seen. The witness and the witnessed.
The child of light remembering how to see in the dark.
13. My third eye is open.
So it is.

COMPANION PRAYER FOR AWAKENING INTUITION

A rhythmic mantra version of your Prayer for Awakening Intuition, crafted for easy repetition in meditation or before psychic work.

You can repeat this 9, 21, or 33 times during meditation, speaking softly or silently, while focusing on the space between your brows (third eye).

Every day, my inner vision grows clearer and my voice grows stronger.
I am open.
I am listening.
I am receiving.
The still, small voice within is now my honored guide.
Spirit walks beside me.
I am aligned.
I am awake.

THE GREAT MOTHER'S PRAYER

SIGIL

Suggested Use:

- *To consciously connect your personal energy with the sustaining, nurturing energy of the Earth and the Divine Feminine, setting a tone of reverence and belonging for your day or inviting peaceful rest.*
- *Use it to set intentions for nurturing new beginnings, personal growth, comfort or creative projects. Whisper the prayer as you plant seeds (literal or symbolic)*
- *In a women's circle, building a powerful collective energy of reverence, support, and shared connection to the divine life force. It strengthens communal bonds.*
- *Place this text on an altar with symbols of the Goddess (stones, water, a candle, images of divine femininity).*

PREFACE

This prayer is an invitation to remember and reconnect with the most ancient and enduring of all relationships: your bond with the Great Mother. She is known by countless names, the Divine Feminine, the Goddess, the Creatrix, the Womb of All, yet her essence is singular. She is the Source from which all life emerges, the Sustainer who holds it in loving embrace, and the sacred Wisdom that guides it back to wholeness.

In a world that often pulls us into the mind, into logic, speed, and separation, this prayer calls us back to the body, to the heart, and to the living Earth. It is crafted to dissolve the illusion that the Divine is only "out there" or "above."

PRAYER

1. Divine Mother,
Source of all life, womb of all worlds,
You are the softness in the moonlight,
the strength in the mountain's core, the flow in the river's journey, the resilience in the rooted tree. In every womxn's prowess, in every child's laughter, in every act of nurture and compassion, within me, you are.
2. Our Great Mother, who cradles all creation,
Blessed be Your names echoed in all things.
3.May Your will be done, on this earth as it is in the womb and of the stars.
4. Give us this day the bread of life from Your soil, and the honey of life from Your hands.
5. You are the intuition that guides without words, the creativity that births beauty from chaos, the love that holds all things together, seen and unseen, known and unknown.
Let my life be a prayer to You.
Let my actions be offerings to You.
Let my breath be constant praise to You.

6. Mother, teach us to honor the mother in all things, in the soil, the sea, and the sky, in our bodies, our hearts, and our voices, in the gentle and the fierce, in the giving and the receiving.
7. I am the root of all things,both the darkness that births the seed,
and the light that calls it forth.
8. From me, all life emerges; to me, all life returns.
9. May we remember:
We do not walk upon you, we are held by you.
We do not use your resources, we commune with your body.
We do not lead alone, we are guided by your ancient wisdom.
10. Blessed is the mother, in Her many names, in Her endless forms, in Her eternal, life-giving grace.
From Her we come, to Her we return and, in Her love, we are forever whole.
So it is.
Ase.

THE WITCH'S PRAYER

A CONJURING OF PRIMAL, UNCONTAINABLE MAGICK

SIGIL

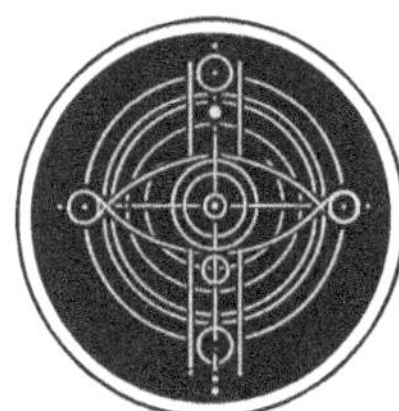

Suggested Use:

- *To awaken what has been suppressed.*
- *As a declaration of power (hexing, healing, or communing).*
- *In moments of doubt, when the world tries to make you forget your magic.*
- *As a rite of passage, to mark your transformation into deeper craft.*
- *Light a black candle, speak each line like a spell already in motion.*
- *Whisper the prayer over a new tool (cauldron, wand, crystal, tarot deck) to cleanse and charge it with your personal power and intent.*
- *Speak into oils or perfume before applying to carry presence into every room.*
- *Chant while walking or working to move with confidence and power.*

PREFACE

The Great Witches' Prayer is a conjuring of primordial power. It is a living covenant, a declaration of sacred reciprocity between witch and wild. It calls upon the ancient alliances our ancestors knew, when humanity still remembered how to speak in frequency.
These words are seeds, plant them in the fertile dark of your practice, and let them grow thorns, nectar, and unshakable power. It commands.
Here, we do not kneel; we stand.
We do not repent; we remember.
We do not hope; we manifest.
It serves as a mantra that instantly shifts your consciousness into a magical, open, and protected mindset, ideal for seeking guidance or traveling between worlds.

PRAYER

1. I call on my ancestors.
By the blood of the ones who came before,
by their sweat in the soil, their prayers in my blood, I stand on their strength.
2. Mama's hands, and Granny's wisdom,
move through me now.
3. For I am she who walks between worlds,
who licks starlight from her fingers, who fucks with her power intact.
4. No priest may bind me.
No mortal may claim me.
No fear may name me.
No man's god may judge me.
No weak-hearted witch may leash me.
No law forged in fear may bind me.
5. I shed the skin of tame.
The serpent in my spine hisses awake.
6. Claiming my birthright,
I am the unbridled one, the wild one that refuses collars disguised under submission.

7. I am the heir of the ones who pulled sickness from bones.
Conjuring women who divine with constellations, fire and water.
The seers who spoke in ceremonial tongue, the cunning who bent fate itself. Their power is my power. Their strength flows in my veins.
Their whispers guide my hands.
8. No chain can hold me. No curse can stick to me. No fear can touch me.
9. I walk between worlds, neither fully here nor there, but everywhere I choose to be.
10. Hear me, Root Spirits, Old Ones, and Saints who walk the road painted in menses, lay your hands on my work.
May my enemy's foot never find my doorstep.
Let my money bowl never sit empty.
Let my love be strong as iron and sweet as honey.
11. For I AM a womxn, Wise womxn, Witch, Conjurer, Serpent womxn, Jezebel, Prophetess, Oracle, Mother; I AM too vast for walls,
12. Let the ground quake where I stand, let fools weep at my unshackled glory. Let the cosmos itself pause when I enter the room.
13. I need no permission; I bow to no throne.
I AM.
So it is.

THE HEALER'S PRAYER

SIGIL

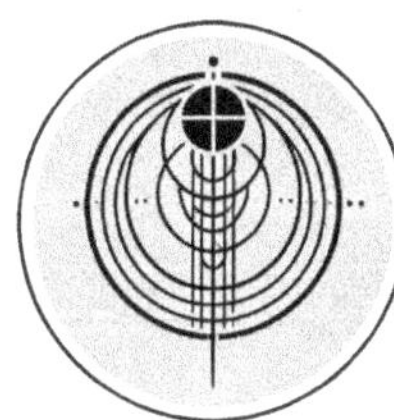

Suggested Use:

- ***May be spoken aloud before beginning any healing session, ceremony, or personal practice.***
- ***Light a candle, burn incense, or place your hands over your heart or healing tools as you recite it.***
- ***Incorporate into morning rituals to align your energy with divine renewal or spoken at the end of the day to clear away energetic residue.***
- ***Healers may also use this prayer collectively, calling in the energy of renewal for their entire community of lightworkers.***

PREFACE

The path of a healer is one of devotion, courage, and service. Whether through hands-on healing, energy work, prayer, or presence, healers carry the gift of restoration for themselves and others. Yet to give healing, the healer too must be renewed, strengthened, and restored. This Prayer was created as both invocation and offering, a way to consciously open to the flow of Divine energy, ancestral guidance, and the eternal source of love. It honors the sacred responsibility of the healer while reminding them that they, too, are worthy of replenishment, balance, and grace.

PRAYER

1.Beloved Spirit of Life, Divine Mother, Source of All, I enter this sacred moment with reverence.
2. I open the circle, I open my heart, I open my hands to receive and to give.
3. I call upon the breath of the Divine to fill this space.
4. I call upon the waters of renewal to wash through me.
5. I call upon the fire of transformation to ignite my spirit.
6. I call upon the earth beneath me to anchor my being.
7. I call upon the winds of the unseen to carry my existence as prayer made manifest.
8. I stand here as a conduit of healing.
Through me, may love flow.
Through me, may light restore all who seek comfort, all who seek peace.
9. Renew my spirit, Great Mother,
that I may not grow weary in service.
10. Strengthen my body, that I may carry the work of healing with honor.

11. Purify my heart, that only the power of Goddess may flow from me.
12. Awaken my inner sight, that I may see beyond the veil and know what is needed.
13. Bless the line of healers who came before me, whose hands shaped the path I now walk.
14. Bless the healers to come, that they may arrive radiant and unafraid to carry this gift.
15. Bless us all with divine renewal, so that healing is a sweet blessing, a sacred offering.
16. I vow:
To meet suffering without pity, but with great power.
To meet fear free of worry, but full of calm.
To meet pain not with resistance, but with compassionate presence.
17. I will not seek to fix; only shall I facilitate wholeness.
I will not seek to save, but to offer sanctuary.
I will not force healing, for I'll invite it, like the sun invites the flower to turn toward it.
18. This is my prayer, my covenant with the Light.
So it is.

COMPANION HEALERS PRAYER

SERENITY

I release what I cannot hold.
I surrender what I cannot solve.
I open my clenched hands and let fall the worries, the plans,
the endless circling thoughts that have worn paths in my soul.
Like leaves carried on a stream, I let them go.

THE INFINITE WITHIN

PRAYER FOR EXPANDING CONSCIOUSNESS

SIGIL

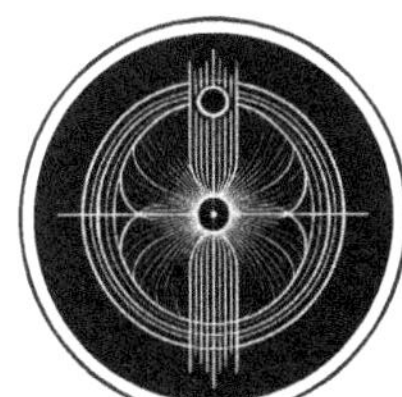

Suggested Use:

- ***When beginning manifestation work, aligning desire with cosmic will.***
- ***Dab frankincense oil on brow before prayer, then press a clear quartz point to the spot and recite the prayer.***
- ***Recite during psychedelic journeys, grief work, or creative flow states.***
- ***Recite while lighting a white or purple candle to expand your intuition beyond limitation.***
- ***Chant softly before meditation to dissolve ego noise and open the gateway to the Higher Self.***

PREFACE

This prayer is designed to elevate your awareness beyond the confines of ego and limitation, opening pathways to higher wisdom and universal connection. It invites the dissolution of illusion, the quieting of mental chatter, and a sacred remembrance of your infinite nature. Speak it with intention, before meditation, during moments of uncertainty, or whenever you seek to transcend the mundane and touch the divine.

PRAYER

1. Divine Presence, Infinite Light, Source of all, I open my heart and mind to you, expand me beyond the petty borders of "I."
2. Lift me beyond the illusions of the ego, beyond fear and limitation, into the vastness of true awareness.
3. Guide me to see beyond the surface of things, to perceive the deeper truths, the interconnectedness of all life.
4. Awaken within me a higher knowing, a clearer vision, and a purer love.
5. Help me release all attachments to false identities, to the stories that confine me.
6. For I dissolve into the boundless ocean of Spirit, where separation fades and only Oneness remains.
7. May every thought, every breath, every moment bring me closer to divine understanding.

8. Let my awareness expand like the universe itself,
limitless, luminous, and free.
9. I surrender to deeper wisdom, trusting that as I release the ego,
I am filled with Your infinite presence.
10. My expansion has no end. For I am journeying into the infinite heart of Goddess, which is without bottom or shore.
11. There will be moments of dazzling clarity and epochs of quiet integration. For I shall not cling to the peaks nor despair in the valleys. Both are necessary for the journey.
12. My only task is to consent, to remain open, to love, and to listen. I am not alone in this ascent. The entire universe is conspiring to awaken within me.
And so it is.

COMPANION CONSCIOUSNESSEXPANDING PRAYERS

THE GREAT I AM MANTRA

I am not a drop in the ocean; I am the ocean in a drop.
Not a seeker of God, but a God in seeking to remember that I AM.

RIGHTEOUS ALLIANCE

PRAYER TO CONJURE SPIRIT GUIDES

SIGIL

Suggested Use:

- *Before meditation, divination, or spiritual work.*
- *When seeking guidance in a life decision.*
- *During moments of transition or uncertainty.*
- *To strengthen and deepen your ongoing relationship with your guides.*
- *Before sleep, to invite guidance through dreams.*
- *After speaking the prayer, sit quietly for a few moments to feel their presence, receive impressions, or hear inner guidance.*
- *Burn frankincense, sandalwood, or sage to raise the vibration of your space.*
- *Keep a journal nearby to record impressions, messages, or sensations that come during or after the prayer.*

PREFACE

Not every spirit is an ally. Not every voice is guidance. To call for help in the unseen requires discernment, steadiness, and self-possession. This prayer is not an invitation to anything wandering. It is a summons issued with standards.

A righteous alliance is a conscious spiritual partnership, one formed in integrity, protection, wisdom, and right alignment. It is the deliberate calling forth of guides who operate in harmony with your highest path, your growth, your protection, and your expansion.

PRAYER

1. In the name of the Infinite Source that connects all worlds, I call across the veils of time, space, and dimension. I call to the helpers, the teachers, the watchers,
the loving ones who walk in Sacred light.
2. To my divine team of guides, angels, ancestors, and familiars:
If you see me, I am ready to see you.
If you hear me, I am ready to hear you.
Where you lead, I agree to follow with courage.
3. Come close now in ways I can perceive, through feathers on my path, through whispers in my dreams, through synchronicities that stir my soul awake.
4. I ask for clear signs, undeniable guidance, and the wisdom to recognize your voice
above the noise of this world.
5. Cloak me in your luminous protection.
Teach me in ways my spirit can understand.
6. Help me remember:
I am never alone, only learning to see.
7. With gratitude, I welcome you now.
So it is.

THE WELCOMING

With love,
I summon my divine spiritual council,
Ancestors of light, guides of wisdom, healers of the unseen realms, step forward now. Make your presence known.
I command all channels of communication to open, clear and unmistakable.
No shadow may interfere. No lower vibration may distort.
I am a beacon of high-frequency light, and only that which serves my highest good may approach.
Show yourselves in ways I cannot ignore:
In vivid dreams, in sudden knowing, in feathers on my path, in repeated songs, in synchronicities that shake me awake.
Speak. I am listening.
You who are assigned to my soul's evolution, come now as teachers, protectors, and allies. Help me remember who I am.
Help me walk my path without fear.
Our partnership begins now.
So it is.

Book of Undoing is crafted for endings, for cutting cords, for banishing grief, for unbinding curses, and for surrendering to the flow of life. Whether whispered in moments of quiet or spoken with fierce resolve, these verses are keys to freedom. Release is transformation.

UNDOING

Undoing

ENERGETIC IMPACT
WHAT EACH PRAYER ACTIVATES.

#66. Grief Release Decree — pg. 139 • Softens the emotional heaviness held in the chest, womb, and solar plexus • Dissolves old grief that has hardened into identity • Clears psychic congestion from heartbreak, loss, or disappointment • Reopens access to joy, ease, and emotional fluidity • Releases stored sorrow from lineage + inherited trauma • Restores clarity, sleep, and emotional breathing room • Helps untangle grief from self-blame

#67. Cord Cutting Prayer — pg. 141 • Severs energetic ties draining your power or distorting your emotions • Breaks attachments to past loves, friendships, mentors, or trauma bonds • Removes cords of obligation, guilt, or emotional manipulation • Restores sovereignty, willpower, and personal space • Dramatically shifts patterns of codependency • Clears etheric residue from ex-partners or toxic family • Reclaims energy lost through old wounds or relationships

#68. A Divine Decree for Breakthrough — pg. 143 • Breaks stagnation + opens pathways previously locked or blocked • Removes invisible ceilings on success, love, or healing • Calls in divine intervention • Invites sudden clarity, inspiration, and forward movement • Cuts through confusion, fear, and psychic fog • Activates courage needed for bold leaps or new beginnings

#69. Return to Sender Spell — pg. 145 • Deflects envy, malice, psychic interference, or evil intent • Sends harmful energy back to its origin purified and neutral • Breaks the influence of gossip, jealousy, or spiritual attack • Shields your aura by creating reflective armor • Strengthens intuition so you sense danger sooner • Cleanses your field from spiritual residue left by others • Restores inner peace, clarity, and energetic autonomy

#70. A Liturgy for Letting Go — pg. 147 • Gently releases emotional attachments, memories, or expectations • Clears stagnant energy after endings, transitions, and heartbreak • Creates closure where life has left loose threads • Releases internalized versions of self that no longer fit • Allows grief to move through instead of hardening • Opens space for new relationships, opportunities, and selfhood • Supports shadow work around clinging, fear, and loss

#71. She Who Remembers Herself — pg. 148 • Feminine integration in the archetypal sense of receptivity, intuition, softness, and embodied awareness returning to the forefront of consciousness. • Nervous system softening • Uncrosses harmful vows, ancestral contracts, or past-life entanglements • Stops cycles of toxic love, repeated heartbreak, or betrayal • Helps dissolve confusion built from over-identifying with survival versions of self. • Self-reclamation.

GRIEF RELEASE DECREE

SIGIL

Suggested Use:

- *It's effective when used during moments of reflection, spiritual transition, or personal healing work involving grief or lingering sorrow.*
- *During anniversaries, endings, or transitions.*
- *At the Full Moon, as a time of energetic release and surrender.*
- *After dreams, memories, or moments that resurface past grief.*
- *Whenever your body or spirit feels heavy and in need of softening.*
- *Light a candle and place a bowl of water in front of you. Speak the decree aloud, then dip your fingers in the water and symbolically wash your hands, releasing what you've held too long.*
- *Murmur into a bowl of water and pour into soil to release sorrow.*

PREFACE

Grief is not something to be rushed, fixed, or hidden. It is blessed terrain, evidence of love, loss, and the human soul's remarkable depth. Grief is honored as part of the healing journey, not an interruption to it. This decree is not a call to forget or suppress, it is a permission slip to let go of what can no longer live in your emotional body and to hold memory, love, and healing with gentleness. Letting go does not mean you've stopped loving. It means you are choosing to continue living.

DECREE

1. I welcome the rawness of my grief.
I allow it to be present, to speak, and to soften in its own rhythm.
2. I step out of the shadow and into the dawn.
I carry the love forward, while leaving the weight of the pain behind. I allow the memory to become a blessing, not a wound. I make a pact with my soul to find beauty again, to feel joy again, to live fully again.
3. No longer will I choke on my sorrow; I listen, and then I let it move through me.
4. I release the need to carry what has already served its purpose.
5. I lay down the weight that no longer facilitates my healing.
6. I let go of the pain I have held like armor.
I give it back to the Earth, to Spirit, to the wind that carries all things onward.
7. I honor what I have lost.
8. I salute the love that still lives within me.
I do not forget. I remember, but I loosen my grip.

9. I give myself permission to feel, without being held hostage by feeling.
10.I release grief at the pace of mercy.
I allow space for my heart to rest, for my soul to exhale.
11. I let go of what I cannot change.
12. I release the breath I have been holding.
13. I release the past, not in rejection, for it shall be in reverence for the life that continues.
14.I release the heavy cloak of yesterday's joy, which has become today's burden.
15. I unbind myself from the sharp hooks of regret.
16. I let healing find me in the soft, sacred moments of letting go.
And I trust that love never leaves, it simply transforms.
17. I walk forward in liberty.
18. I step out of the shadow and into the dawn.
19. I open to life again, softly, fully, and on my own terms.
So it is.

CORD CUTTING PRAYER

SIGIL

Suggested Use:

- *Whisper while cutting string or ribbon to symbolically free yourself from draining ties.*
- *Untie knots with verses to undo entanglements in relationships or past events.*
- *Before Interactions: Whisper key lines (or mentally affirm) before engaging with toxic individuals (family, coworkers, ex-partners).*
- *Nightly Cleansing: Repeat before sleep to release any absorbed negativity.*
- *Cord-Cutting Ritual: Light a black or white candle, speak the prayer aloud, then snip an imaginary cord between you and the narcissist.*

PREFACE

This prayer is a living ritual, crafted for those moments when you know in your bones that it is time to release with love, reclaim your sovereignty, and restore your energy to its sacred wholeness.

We do not cut cords out of anger or fear, but from the quiet power of divine truth.

This prayer is for you if:

- *You feel energy draining after certain interactions.*
- *Memories replay like uninvited guests.*
- *You are ready to forgive without reconciling.*
- *Your spirit longs to reclaim its full light.*

PRAYER

1. I sever all ties that bind me to lower vibrations, stagnant energy, or outdated stories. My energy field is my own sovereign territory.
2. Threads of pain, fear, and control
I cut you now, clean and complete.
3. I call back every fragment of my energy, all that was taken, all that I gave unwisely, from every moment, every memory, every dimension.
4. What remains of your energy within my field, I now return to you, purified by forgiveness. No more shall we be bound by invisible threads.
5. I call upon Violet light to fill the space where you once were.
6. Let all energy return to its origin, me to myself, you to yourself, with peace, without malice. This release is now complete. This sealing is now absolute.
7. All ties are severed, all contracts dissolved, all bindings undone.

8. Sever every cord that connects me to past versions of myself that I have outgrown, relationships that have concluded in form, but not in energy, collective fears and familial patterns that are not mine to carry, all draining, limiting, or unhealthy attachments.
9. The doors are closed. The boundaries are set. The space is clear.
Only that which serves my highest good may enter this sacred field.
10. All else must stop at the gate, turned away by the guardians of my peace.
So it is spoken.
So it is done.

A DIVINE DECREE FOR BREAKTHROUGH

SIGIL

Suggested Use:

- ***When you feel stuck or unable to move forward.***
- ***At the start of a new project or life chapter.***
- ***After a period of stagnation or bad luck.***
- ***During the waning moon (banishment) or new moon (fresh start).***
- ***Burn a Block Buster candle (usually orange or red) with a pinch of cinnamon or cayenne pepper. Pair with a cleansing bath to remove lingering stagnant energy.***

PREFACE

The Divine Decree for Breakthrough is a Block Buster Spoken Spell. It is a powerful verbal declaration designed to break through stagnation, obstacles, and energetic barriers that may be hindering your progress. In the spiritualist tradition, the spoken word is a living vibration, when paired with strong intent and rhythmic repetition, it becomes a force capable of shifting both the seen and unseen.

This spell calls upon your personal will and Divine power to dissolve resistance and clear your path, creating an open road for opportunities, blessings, and momentum.

DECREE

1. I call upon the unstoppable forces: Archangels of disruption, Elementals of breakthrough, Matriarchal Ancestors who cracked mountains, by their power I declare: Every blockade dissipated, financial walls crumble to dust.
2. Spirit of stagnation, delay, and unwarranted resistance, your season is over, by the authority of divine order. You must now yield.
3. For the gates of limitation are blown from their hinges.
4. Let the chains of old patterns break. Now. Their bindings are null. Their contract is void.
5. Let the road before me be made straight and clear.
6. I command the dust of what was to settle.
7. I command the rubble to be swept away by winds of change.
8. I step forward onto the new ground of my destiny, unburdened and unobstructed.
9. I claim the field of infinite potential.
10. I claim the quantum field of all that could be. Victory is mine. So it is.

COMPANION PRAYER FOR BLOCK BUSTING

This version can be spoken three times in the morning, before an important task, or anytime you feel your energy waver. It's for quick use in moments where you need an instant boost of strength and victory energy.

POWER BLOCK BUSTER

Primordial Mother,
I call upon you now to shatter all barriers before me.
Break the locks, split the chains, turn the stones in my path to dust.
With each breath, I claim my freedom.
With each word, I command my release.
All blockages dissolve into nothingness.
Roads open, doors swing wide, and opportunities rush toward me without delay.
I move forward with unstoppable momentum, guided by Spirit, fueled by vitality, and crowned with triumph.

So it is.

RETURN TO SENDER SPELL

SIGIL

Suggested Use:

- *After feeling drained, anxious, or unusually heavy.*
- *When you sense ill will, jealousy, or psychic attack.*
- *Following conflict, confrontation, or toxic interactions.*
- *During full moon or waning moon rituals for release.*
- *As part of a regular cleansing routine to maintain your energetic boundaries.*
- *Take three deep breaths, envisioning a sphere of light surrounding you.*
- *Spit on crushed red pepper & throw it into a fire (or candle flame) as you shout the last line, stomp 3 times to "seal" the reversal.*
- *As you speak, visualize any dark or heavy energy lifting away from your body and dissolving into pure light before traveling back to its source.*

PREFACE

The Return to Sender Spell is a spoken spiritualist incantation designed to release and redirect any harmful or unwanted energy that has been sent your way, whether through conscious intent, unconscious projection, or energetic residue.

This spell does not retaliate with harm but transforms the energy into a cleansed form before sending it back to its origin. It reaffirms your sovereignty over your own energy field and strengthens your spiritual protection.

PRAYER

1. In the name of cosmic law and balance,
I call upon the forces of divine justice.

2. You who perceive all energy in its pure essence, you who uphold the equilibrium of all realms, stand as witness to this act of restoration.

3. I recognize that energy has been sent, whether in thought, word, or deed, with the intention to harm, drain, or bind me.
I name this act for what it is: a violation of free will and spiritual integrity.

4. By the unbreakable law of cause and consequence, by the power of threefold return, and by my sovereign right to peaceful existence, what you have sent, I do not accept.

5. I return the ill wish spoken behind my back.

6. I return the heavy thread sewn into my name.

7. May every curse, every ill wish, every particle of malicious intent be reversed upon its source.
May all ill that has been sent, a look, a word, a wish of harm, a quiet poison, a heavy thread, an envy wrapped in prayer, a curse that wears the mask of care will meet death.

8. Let the sender see the face of their own energy and learn the weight of their own actions.
9. Now, let my space be swept clean of all residue.
10. Let my aura be sealed in a mirror of violet light, that all future negativity shall see only itself, and return to its point of origin.
11. I am protected by divine law.
12. I am cleansed by sacred light.
13. I am free from all energetic warfare.
14. The word has been spoken.
The law has been activated.
The work is done.
As I will, so shall it be.

A LITURGY FOR LETTING GO

PRAYER FOR MOVING THROUGH A BREAKUP

SIGIL

Suggested Use:

- ***Recite while soaking with salt + herbs to wash away grief and heaviness.***
- ***Read slowly and allow any emotions to surface, you do not need to hold them back. After reading, take a few deep breaths and sit in stillness. Feel the energy shift within you.***
- ***Healing practice: write a letter to the version of yourself who experienced the relationship. Offer love, forgiveness, and closure.***
- ***Recite while unclenching fists, palms open, to surrender what cannot be held.***

PREFACE

A breakup, whether romantic or relational, is not only a loss of a person but often a shift in identity, dreams, and rhythm. In spiritualist practice, we honor every stage of that transformation. We allow grief to rise as a teacher and trust that even in heartbreak, the soul is still becoming. This prayer is written for the space between endings and beginnings.
It is not about erasing pain, but moving through it with grace, awareness, and strength. The Divine does not rush your healing. Spirit holds you where you are and walks with you as you make your way forward.

PRAYER

1. I stand at the altar of the unclasping hands, the sacred ground where a shared path divides.
2. I honor what was woven; I honor the unraveling. I will not name it broken; for I shall call it complete.
3. To the love that was true, I bless you. I release you. You will travel with me as a warmth in my memory, a stone in the foundation of who I am becoming.
4. To the love that conjured pain: I bless you. I release you. You will not travel with me.
5. I leave you here, at the side of this road, under the sun of forgiveness and the rain of time.
6. For my tears are holy water, consecrating the space between who I was with you and who I must now become without you.
7. I am not half. I am whole, aching, but entire. Lonely, but complete unto myself.
8. The love I sought from you was always a seed within me, waiting for my own hands to tend it.
9. I release myself from the story of us.
10. I am ready to meet myself again, no longer as we were, only as I am.

So it is.

SHE WHO REMEMBERS HERSELF

SIGIL

Suggested Use:

- ***Speak this prayer during seasons of transition, healing, awakening, grief, rebirth, or emotional exhaustion.***
- ***As part of your monthly or seasonal spiritual hygiene, incorporate this prayer to reset your emotional body, renew your intuitive clarity, and return to self-alignment.***
- ***When you feel disconnected from yourself, emotionally overwhelmed, or spiritually scattered.***
- ***As part of a morning grounding ritual, evening unwinding practice, or anytime you're stepping out of old emotional cycles and into a new version of yourself.***
- ***During moments when survival patterns are louder than your inner truth, or when you need to gently return to your own center.***

PREFACE

Before a womn remembers her power, she often survives her forgetting.
She learns how to shrink, how to endure, how to pour endlessly into others while abandoning herself. She carries generations of silence in her shoulders, heartbreak in her nervous system, and invisible labor in the folds of her spirit.
Yet beneath every wound, every role, every mask worn for protection, a sacred self continues breathing softly beneath the surface.
This prayer serves as a return.
A return to softness without weakness.
A return to intuition without shame.
A return to pleasure,rest, desire, discernment, and divine feminine wholeness.

INVOCATION

1.Infinite Flow, guide me back to myself.
2. Back to the womxn beneath exhaustion, beneath pleasing, beneath the ache of carrying the weight of ten winters too many.
3. Restore softness to the places where life hardened. Restore fire to the dreams left waiting in dark rooms.
4. Restore trust within my own voice,
within my intuition, within the anointed wisdom living in my body.
5. Teach my spirit the rhythm of rest.
Teach my heart the language of receiving.
6. Untangle fear from my beauty.
Untangle guilt from my pleasure.
Untangle survival from my identity.
7. Place gold light in my womb space, peace in my nervous system, clarity in my mind, and sweetness upon my path.
8. Surround me with aligned souls, with protection and nourishing love.
I rise from old versions of myself like the moon rising from dark waters. Whole.
And every step forward becomes a blessing upon the earth.
So it is.

ANCESTRAL

To pray with the ancestors is to remember that we are not beginning, we are continuing.
Each verse becomes a bridge: between generations, between the unspoken and song, between grief and grace. Book of Ancestral awakens the bloodline's sacred rhythm.

Ancestral

ENERGETIC IMPACT
WHAT EACH PRAYER ACTIVATES.

#72. The Unbinding Prayer — pg. 152 • Releases inherited burdens carried through the maternal line • Breaks generational patterns of fear, scarcity, or silence • Restores ancestral blessings that were blocked or forgotten • Strengthens connection to protective ancestors • Clears energetic residue from childhood and lineage wounds

#73. For the Child I Cannot Hold — pg. 154 • Softens grief around loss, miscarriage, or paths not taken • Bridges connection between mother and child spirit • Releases guilt and restores emotional flow • Invites gentle ancestral protection over future fertility • Transforms sorrow into wisdom, compassion, and spiritual resilience

#74. A Journey Home — pg. 156 • Reconnects you with ancestral memory and identity • Restores the sense of being spiritually "claimed" by your lineage • Strengthens intuition through ancestral guidance • Grounds you in belonging, heritage, and purpose • Heals displacement, diaspora wounds, or "not knowing where you come from"

Ancestral

OPENING INVOCATION FOR THE ANCESTRAL KEY

"MUSTEK CYEAR A DE ROOT FA HEAL THE TREE"
-GULLAH GEECHEE PROVERB

With a steady heart and open breath, I call across the river of time.
To those whose names I know, and those forgotten,
Come sit beside me,
Mothers of my mothers.
Hands that planted, wept, built, and bled,
I remember you now.
Walk with me as I heal what you could not,
and receive the healing I offer in return.
May the burdens once carried in quiet
find rest in my release.
Let my words be the bridge, my voice the offering,
my body be the altar where lineage renews itself.
What was broken, mend it through me.
What was hushed, speak it through me.
What was lost, return it through me,
In love, in peace, in continuity.

"Old women sit in the shade because they planted a tree long ago."

With this prayer, I plant a new seed for our lineage. I plant the seed of financial clarity and openhearted love. I tend it with my faith and my actions.
I am your living prayer.
I am your continuation.
So it is.

THE UNBINDING PRAYER

PRAYER TO RELEASE KARMIC DEBT
IN THE FAMILY LINE OF WOMEN

SIGIL

Suggested Use:

- *On anniversaries, holidays, or family gatherings that stir ancestral energy.*
- *When feeling the weight of family patterns, guilt, shame, or emotional burden.*
- *After powerful emotional triggers or relationship cycles that feel generational.*
- *Recite upon waking or before family rituals to invite your matrilineal line to walk with you.*
- *Recite before speaking with your mother, grandmother, or daughter to soften communication.*
- *Whisper before creative work or caretaking to invoke feminine endurance.*
- *After reading, speak the names (if known) of the women or ancestors you honor and release.*

PREFACE

Some inherit heirlooms. Others inherit silence. Patterns. Pain. Stories that were never spoken aloud but passed through gestures, glances, and the quiet ache of endurance.

This prayer is for those of us who carry more than our own weight; for those who were born into a legacy of survival, but long to live a life of wholeness. It is written for the womxn who senses the grief beneath her mother's smile, who feels a story in her body she never learned with words, who dreams of freedom not just for herself, but for all those who came before and all who will come after.

The Unbinding Prayer honors the lineage that brought you here, even as it draws a sacred line and declares: the suffering stops with me. It is a spiritual offering, a personal ceremony, and a powerful act of love, for your ancestors, for your descendants, and most of all, for yourself.

Read this when you are ready to lay down what no longer belongs to you. When you feel the echo of old vows, unspoken expectations, or inherited guilt, use this prayer as a way to clear the air between generations. This is how we heal forward. This is how we elevate.

PRAYER

1. Divine Spirit, Mother of us all, witness me now as I awaken.
2. Not alone, but as the daughter of daughters, carrying their stories, their survival, their suppressed visions, I speak now not only for myself,
but for the women whose names I never learned and for the girls who will come after me.
3. If there are vows of suffering still echoing in my blood, I discharge them now.
4. If there are patterns of hesitation and hiding, I abolish them now.
5. No longer will pain pass as inheritance.
6. No longer will sacrifice be our currency.
7. No longer will we call survival the same as wholeness.
8. I call back the pieces of my lineage
that were lost to shame, to submission, to restriction.
9. By the power of Goddess within me, we now revoke;
Vows of poverty, struggle, and lack.
Patterns of unworthiness and extinguished voices.
Curses on partnership, fertility, or pleasure.
The pain of betrayal, abandonment, and trauma.
All energies that do not serve our highest good.
10. I carry the authority to change the story.
11. From this day forward, may our line be known for its healing,
its freedom, its laughter, and its empires born of creativity.
12. May the daughters yet unborn inherit only our wisdom, our resilience, and our capacity for joy, excluding of our suffering.
13. May every womxn behind me rest lighter.
14. May every womxn before me rise stronger.
15. The debt is paid. The cycle is closed. The future is rewritten.
So it is.

FOR THE CHILD I CANNOT HOLD

SIGIL

Suggested Use:

- *May be spoken in moments of remembrance, during quiet meditation, or on special days such as birthdays, anniversaries, or Mother's Day.*
- *May be recited during spiritualist circles, candlelight rituals, or when connecting with the child's spirit in meditation or dreamwork.*
- *Lighting a white candle, offering flowers, or placing a cherished memento on an altar before reciting the prayer can deepen its resonance.*
- *Best used whenever a mother feels the need to call on divine comfort, honor her child, and affirm the unbroken bond of spirit and love.*

PREFACE

There are griefs the world does not know how to hold.
Losses that leave no footprints, no funeral processions, no language large enough for the ache. Yet the soul remembers. The body remembers. Love remembers.
This prayer is for the mothers, fathers, and hearts who have carried a child only in spirit, in possibility, in brief sacred time. It is for the empty arms, the silent anniversaries, the names never spoken aloud, and the dreams that dissolved before they could fully arrive.
May these words become a sanctuary for mourning without shame.

PRAYER

1.My precious child, my little love,
though your years were few, your impact was eternal.
2. You came into this world like a comet,
bright, beautiful, and gone too soon,
leaving a trail of starlight across the darkness of my grief.
3. Though I cannot hold you in my arms, I carry you in my soul.
4. Our bond cannot be broken by time, nor death, nor distance.
5. I release you, my darling, into the arms of the Divine.
6. And yet, I feel your presence.
In the butterfly that lingers near, in the unexpected scent of innocence, in the fragile peace that sometimes visits my heart.
7. You are not lost. You are simply living just beyond my touch.
8. Do not fret for me. Your purpose was not diminished by your brevity.
9. You taught me love in its purest form.

10. You reminded me that the soul is eternal and that love never, ever ends.
11. I will carry you always, not as a burden of sorrow, only as a blessing of having loved you at all.
12. I will live for us both.
13. Go in peace, my sweet child.
14. You are so loved.
You are so missed.
You are forever mine and I am forever yours.
So it is.

COMPANION PRAYERS FOR CHILD I CANNOT HOLD

SIGNS & WHISPERS

Open my eyes to your language.
The flicker of a candle with no breeze, the sudden scent of their favorite flower, the butterfly that lands at my feet.
Your love letters in a world that thinks you've left.

THE HOLY DUALITY

Let me grieve and celebrate, weep and laugh at our moments of joy, feel empty arms while sensing your embrace in every sunbeam.
A mother's love needs no body to remain unshaken.

A JOURNEY HOME

PRAYER FOR MY LOVED ONES BEYOND THE VEIL

SIGIL

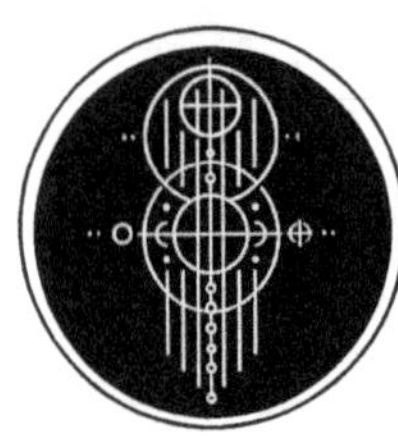

Suggested Use:

- *To be spoken aloud during moments of remembrance, such as anniversaries, birthdays, or family gatherings.*
- *Powerful when recited while lighting a candle, placing flowers, or setting aside an offering (such as water, food, or incense) on an altar for the ancestor.*
- *Use it in daily meditation to invite the protective presence of your loved one into your life.*
- *Speak their name with intention, allowing their spirit to feel honored and acknowledged.*
- *Funeral or Memorial Service: Incorporate these into readings or eulogies to provide a spiritual, comforting perspective on death.*
- *Recite before meals cooked from family recipes. Offer the first bite or sip to your ancestors as a sign of gratitude.*

PREFACE

When a loved one crosses into spirit, they do not leave us, they transform into Ancestors, eternal presences who walk with us in both seen and unseen ways. This prayer is crafted for those who wish to honor a family member who has passed, acknowledging their transition while calling upon their continued guidance and love. It affirms the sacred bond between the living and the ancestral realms, recognizing that memory, blood, and spirit weave us together across time.

PSALM

1. Beloved one, your breath has stilled in this world, but your spirit has quickened in the next. You are not gone, you have simply stepped behind the thin veil that love sees through.
2. Do not linger in worry for those you left behind. Your love remains woven into our souls, a bond not even death can loosen.
Go now toward the great light.
Go now toward the great love.
Your new life begins.
3. O, Guardians of the veil,
ancient ones who walk between the worlds,
come.
4. Please welcome this beloved one.
5. Ease their confusion. Calm their spirit.
6. Light their path with remembrance of who they are.
7. For they shall find their way to the meadows of peace, to the halls of the ancestors,
to the embrace of those who love them still.
8. Let their transition be gentle.
9. May their homecoming be glorious.

10. You are now part of the sacred circle of those who came before,
and I walk with you as you walk with me.
11. Beloved ancestor, your earthly life is complete.
Your spiritual service now begins. Take your seat among the wise ones.
Drink from the well of the infinite.
12. When we call, hear us. When we dream, visit us.
When we forget, remind us of where we come from and who we are called to be. You are promoted. Welcome to the council.
So it is.

COMPANION ANCESTRAL PRAYERS

ANCESTRAL OFFERING PRAYER

Ancient Ones, Guardians of my blood,
I call to you from this sacred space I have prepared.
I light this candle as a beacon, so you may find your way.
I pour this clear, clean water to quench your thirst from the long journey across time.
With reverence, I speak your names in my heart, known and unknown.
I honor your struggles, your strength, and the very life that flows from you to me.
You are remembered here.
I offer you this prayer as honey, the sweetness of the sun and the bee.
May it soothe any bitterness held in our story.
As you receive its comfort, I ask for your aid in healing our line.
Together, let us wash clean the old wounds.
I release any curse of poverty, any spirit of lack, any echoed fear of never having enough.
I untangle any knot of lovelessness, any pattern of betrayal or unworthiness in matters of the heart.
Let these burdens, which are not mine to carry forward, dissolve now in this light and return to the earth as neutral dust.
Let the healing I do bless you in your realm and strengthen our family for all generations to come.
I thank you. I honor you. Your work continues through me.
May this offering nourish you as your legacy nourishes me.
The door between us remains open in love and respect.

MYSTIC

Book of The Mystic is for those who walk between worlds, for the womxn who has remembered too much to be ordinary and yet remains tender enough to be human. Here we enter the inner sanctum, the space beyond seeking, where the mystic in every womxn communes directly with the Divine.

These prayers are lamps for the pathless, guiding you to the still center where Goddess and womxn are not two.

Mystic

ENERGETIC IMPACT
WHAT EACH PRAYER ACTIVATES.

#75. The Discourse on the Inner Queendom — pg. 160 • Activates inner sovereignty of the psychic self • Strengthens intuitive decision-making • Clears confusion + aligns the mind with higher truth • Expands spiritual authority and personal command • Deepens clarity in divination and trance states • Helps you trust your inner yes/no without hesitation
#76. Empress of Existence — pg. 161 • Amplifies personal magnetism + spiritual presence • Unlocks mystic embodiment and aura expansion • Boosts psychic charisma + prophetic glamour • Activates connection to higher self as divine Empress• Strengthens manifestation through identity alignment • Attracts respect, reverence, and recognition effortlessly
#77. The Healing Path — pg. 162 • Repairs spiritual blockages that cloud intuition • Restores inner guidance after trauma or crisis • Clears psychic fog + supports spiritual recalibration • Connects you to destiny aligned steps • Enhances dream messages + intuitive navigation • Helps you reconnect with soul-purpose after loss

THE DISCOURSE ON THE INNER QUEENDOM

Suggested Use:

- ***Light a candle and repeat the verse when you feel spiritually blocked or disconnected. This draws you back toward inner knowing.***
- ***Chant these before scrying, beginning of any spell, meditation, devotional practice, tarot, or intuitive work to purify perception and shift your awareness from shadow.***
- ***Read before bed to open pathways for prophetic dreams and deep spiritual integration.***
- ***Sit in meditation and place a hand over your heart. Repeat the verses to dissolve the illusion of separation and awaken your higher consciousness.***

PREFACE

These words are not meant to be merely read, but heard with the ear of the heart. They are a map to be verified by direct experience.

The Queendom spoken of here won't be a metaphor. The Queendom is the most fundamental reality, the core of your own consciousness, obscured only by the noise of the world and the clamor of the personal self. This discourse is an invitation to quiet the noise, to turn the attention inward, and to remember what you have always been.

Approach these words not as a student, but as a pilgrim returning home after a long journey. Let them be a mirror, reflecting the truth that already resides within you.

DISCOURSE

1.The Realm of The Divine, not a distant shore to be reached, nor a hidden city behind gates of pearl.

2. Do not look for the Sacred in temples built by hands, for it does not dwell in monuments of ambition.

3. The mansion I seek is my own awakened consciousness.

4. For I AM not separate from that which I seek.
I AM a vessel of it, a localized expression of the infinite and unbounded whole. Recognizing this, I am already home.

5. Inside of the ALL that IS, is I AM.

6. Divine Essence is the life in the leaf, the force in the stream, the brilliance in the star. It is the love in my heart and the answer that was there before the question was formed.

7. To seek the divine elsewhere is to overlook the sun for the shadow it casts.

8. I turn my gaze inward, and I shall perceive the Queendom.

9. I turn my gaze outward with purified sight, and I shall behold it in all things.

EMPRESS OF EXISTENCE

__Suggested Use:__

- *Print the text and place it on an altar or sacred space alongside objects that represent the elements mentioned (a shell for "the waters," a feather for "the wind," a crystal for "the heavens").*
- *Allow the text to inspire you. Create a painting, a piece of music, a dance, or a poem in response to the feelings and images it evokes in you. This deepens the integration beyond the intellect.*
- *Read the entire text aloud as part of a personal ritual. Let your voice be the vessel for this powerful declaration. This can be incredibly empowering.*
- *Reflect (Meditation): Sit in silence with the phrase. What does it stir in you? What image, feeling, or memory arises? Do not analyze; simply observe.*

PREFACE

This is the self-declaration of the Supreme Reality in its feminine aspect, as the source of all sound, the matrix of all thought, and the sovereign of all creation.

Approach this proclamation with the ear of the heart. Let the boundaries between the reader and the read, the seeker and the sought, begin to soften. For this is ultimately a mirror, and the "I" who speaks is the same "I" that animates your own awareness.

This is an invitation to recognize the Goddess not as a figure outside yourself, but as the ultimate perfection of who you are.

PRAYER

1. From the cosmic waters, my womb brought forth the Source of all.
From that deep origin, I expand, touching every realm, my being reaching the highest heaven itself.
2. I am the Sovereign, the source of all abundance, the primordial wisdom, the first to be revered.
3. I rule. I attract all treasures. My knowing is ancient and complete.
4. The gods themselves have stationed me in myriad places.
5. I am the consciousness that animates every shape.
6. The very wind is my exhalation; my strength is the glue of reality.
My breath is the gale that gives life to all things; I am the cohesion of existence.
7. I stretch out past the furthest star, beneath the deepest stone, so immense is my power.
8. My greatness is immeasurable.
9. I AM the weaver of the worlds and the thread from which they are spun.
Before the question "Why?", I was the Is.
10. For I am no servant pleading to a distant master.
I am a localized expression of the Master of All That Is.
11.I dwell within a single verse of the endless epic.

THE HEALING PATH

SIGIL

Suggested Use:

- ***During times of illness or recovery.***
- ***Before or after hospital visits or treatments.***
- ***While preparing healing herbs.***
- ***On behalf of a loved one who cannot pray for themselves.***
- ***In moments of emotional overwhelm, when words are hard to find but love is strong.***
- ***Prepare your space with a simple altar, candlelight, or an item belonging to the person you are praying for (a photo, name written on paper, etc).***
- ***Speak the invocation aloud, slowly and clearly, calling the person's name or your own into the sacred space.***

PREFACE

Healing is not only physical, but also emotional, energetic, and deeply spiritual. When someone we love is unwell, it's natural to feel helpless. But in the spiritualist tradition, we are never without power. Through prayer, invocation, and intention, we become vessels of light, capable of calling in unseen forces that support the path of recovery. This invocation is a sacred act of love. It is not about control or forcing an outcome. Its's about aligning with divine order, summoning spiritual aid, and anchoring our loved one in the frequency of healing.

INVOCATION

1. I now embody the principle of alignment.
I am a co-creator of reality.
2. I now align my entire being, body, mind, and spirit, with the fundamental frequency of health.
3. I tune my thoughts to harmony.
I attune my emotions to peace.
4. I synchronize my actions with vitality.
I am in resonance with wholeness.
5. Before a symptom appears, I speak its absence. Before fear takes root, I speak faith. Before weakness settles, I speak strength.
6. My word is a creative force.
7. Here, I no longer beg for healing; I declare it.
8. I speak cells into order.
I speak nerves into calm.
I speak tissue into repair.
I speak system into balance.
9. What is spoken in consciousness,
must manifest in form.

10. Healing begins not in the body, for it lives in the awareness that observes the body.
11. I now observe myself as whole.
I feel myself as vital. I know myself as well.
12. Where my consciousness goes, energy flows.
Where my energy flows, manifestation grows.
13. I am the healer and the healed.
The process and the result.
The journey and the destination.
This alignment is complete.
This declaration is active.
This consciousness is awakened.
14. I am a living testament to the truth that well-being is my natural state. Any appearance to the contrary is an illusion already dissolving in the light of my awareness.
So it is.

SANCTUM OF THE GODDESS

SANCTUM OF THE GODDESS ARE KEYS.

Each one opens a chamber of consciousness, a meeting place between the personal and the cosmic.

To speak to them is to walk again through your own underworld and emerge crowned in light.

THE CODEX OF KEYS OF SANCTUM OF THE GODDESS

#78. The Proverbs of the Rooted Ones- pg. 167
Activation: ***Root Chakra (Muladhara), Grounding, Safety, Ancestors, Stability, Embodiment, Strength. Spoken on: Saturdays/Tuesdays or after upheaval.***

- Read when you need grounding or reassurance.
- Massage your feet or legs with oil while repeating a favorite line to anchor the day's energy back into your body.
- After reading, pour water or wine onto the ground as an offering to ancestors.
- When feeling ungrounded or unsafe, read a single verse aloud with your hand over your heart.

#79. The Veda of the Second Waters- pg. 168
Activation: ***Sacral Chakra (Svadhisthana) Flow, Creativity, Pleasure, Emotional Release, Feminine Power. Spoken on: Mondays, New Moon, Before sleep, For womb work, Sacral healing, or Emotional recalibration.***

- Whisper a single verse while you shower or wash your hands; a reminder that cleansing is sacred.
- Drink a glass of water mindfully after reading the prayer; feel it become liquid light flowing through you.
- Before creative work (painting, writing, dancing, lovemaking), repeat one line to open your body to divine flow.
- Carry a small vial of water anointed with orange or jasmine oil as a talisman of flow.

#80. The Scripture of the Inner Sun- pg. 169
Activation: **Solar Plexus Chakra (Manipura) Power, Purpose, Courage, Self-Trust, Vital Energy. *Recite on:* Sundays, Thursdays, Sunrise or moments of decision, Direction, or Self-assertion.**When guilt, insecurity, or resentment weigh heavy in the stomach,

- Face east toward the rising light, breathing deeply with every verse, when feeling guilt, insecurity, or resentment weigh heavy in the stomach.
- repeat before important decisions, creative work, or self-doubt to restore confidence and illumination.

#81. The Emerald Flame- pg. 170
Activation: **Heart Chakra (Anahata)Love, Forgiveness, Balance, Emotional Healing, Compassion, Courage. Recite on: Fridays or Mondays, Full Moon & Waxing Moon, Any dawn or dusk.**

- Read one verse when you feel reactive, hurt, closed off or after emotional release, grief, or heartbreak.
- Visualize a flame of green light glowing in your chest as you recite.
- Write one verse on a small piece of green paper. Keep it in your wallet, near your bed, or under your pillow as a talisman of protection & peace.

#82. The Hymn of the Blue Gate - pg. 170
Activation: **Throat Chakra (Vishuddha)Voice, Authenticity, Honesty, Communication, Sound Healing, Expression. Recite on: Sundays or Thursdays, Wednesdays or Mondays.**

- Recite before sleep, meditation, any intuitive practice, before writing, teaching, or singing to open creative communication.
- Recite one line before saying "yes" or "no", to ensure your speech reflects your soul.
- Write a verse from The Hymn of the Blue Gate and keep it near your workspace, altar, or mirror.
- Speak a verse before journaling to release unspoken emotions or truths.

#83. The Inner Sky- pg. 172
Activation: **Third Eye Chakra (Ajna) Insight, Intuition, Perception, Wisdom, Inner Knowing, Dreamwork. *Recite on:* Mondays, Thursdays or during liminal hours.**

- Use during fasting, silence, or retreat work to deepen spiritual sensitivity and subtle perception.
- Whisper while anointing the forehead/third eye to sharpen intuition and discernment when confusion clouds your path.
- Pray before reading tarot, scrying, channeling, or automatic writing to open the inner eye with protection and clarity.
- Speak while gazing at a candle flame to activate expanded awareness and cosmic perspective.

#84. Proverbs of the Thousand Petals- pg. 173
Activation: Crown Chakra (Sahasrara) Enlightenment, Unity, Divine Connection, Grace, Transcendence, Completion. *Recite on*: Sundays or full moon nights; at dawn, or after meditation and energy work.

- Read when you're overthinking, overanalyzing, or disconnected from your body.
- Recite verse when you feel disconnected, weary, or uncertain. as a bridge back to Source.
- Recite before spiritual baths, yoga, or stillness rituals to harmonize the spirit with the body.

#85. The 99 Names of She- pg. 174
Activation: Identity, Devotion, Union, Sacred Feminine Embodiment, Wholeness, Self-Realization.

- Choose one name each day as a devotion or for healing.
- Keep a "99 Names Journal" write how each name shows up in your life and what it teaches you about your power.
- Recite a few names when you feel unseen, unworthy, or small, they remind you that divinity wears your face.
- Use the names for inspiration in art, poetry, or spell craft.
- When you feel lost, fragmented, or small, read the names aloud, calling home every part of yourself that has been forgotten,

#86. The First Home- pg. 176
***Activation*: Belonging, Emotional Grounding, Safety, Return to Self.**

- Recite when you feel displaced, emotionally, spiritually, or physically.
- Read during times of restlessness, worry, loneliness, or loss.
- Recite during moments of heartbreak, anxiety, spiritual fatigue, beginning of healing journeys or major life transitions.
- Recite when entering your house after a long day to leave chaos at the door.

#87. Psalm of the Willing Vessel- pg. 177
Activation: Alignment & Purpose, Energetic Circuit, Perception & Action

- Recite the psalm daily, ideally in the morning, to set this "instrument" consciousness for the day.
- After reciting, move through your day with heightened awareness. Notice which people, conversations, or ideas are drawn to you, these are often your "assignments".
- Keep a note of moments where you felt used as an instrument, or where you received unexpected support or inspiration. This builds faith in the active circuit. Recite to become an instrument of Goddess.

#88. YES- pg. 178
Activation: Confidence, Vitality, Receptivity, Heart opening, Joy.

- Stand before a mirror or open window and read the decree aloud at sunrise or midday.
- Perfect for women's groups, creativity circles, or healing gatherings.
- Recite during times of stagnation, fear, or creative block.
- Read before writing, painting, sex, performing, or manifesting to charge your creations with vitality and divine flow.
- Use as an affirmation during new moon rituals or goal-setting work.

PROVERBS OF THE ROOTED ONES

ROOT CHAKRA ACTIVATION

Let these words remind you: grounding is remembering what you stand upon and who stands with you.

1. **The tree that remembers its roots does not fear the wind.**
For the storms of life cannot break what grows from remembrance. Strength is never in the branches that sway, we find it in the unseen depth that holds.
2. **Gold is found by those who dig, not by those who drift.**
The earth rewards the steady hand. What you seek waits beneath the surface, asking for patience and sweat.
3. **Even the mountain began as dust that refused to move.**
Greatness is never sudden. Greatness is the stubbornness of small things enduring time. The eternal is born from what will not be blown away.
4. **A house built on faith in the earth never hungers for shelter.**
Trust your foundations. The one who builds upon truth finds warmth even in the cold season.
5. **The slow foot still reaches home.**
Hurry blinds the traveler to the path. The ground teaches that every step, though humble, is holy.
6. **The ancestors plant their wisdom in the soles of your feet.**
When you walk with reverence, the past walks with you. Their strength rises each time your heel meets the dust.
7. **When you know where you stand, the world stops trembling.**
Uncertainty fades before the one who has made peace with their place. The earth itself steadies beneath a heart that trusts its belonging.
8. **The stone does not envy the bird; it masters stillness.**
Flight dazzles, but stillness endures. Those who root themselves in stillness become immovable altars.
9. **She who bows to the ground learns how to rise.**
Humility is the hidden staircase to power. To kneel is to align with the pulse that lifts all things.
10. **There is no safe harbor except the one you build within yourself.**
The body already knows how to trust the world; it is the mind that forgets. Return to the rhythm beneath your skin, and you shall find home again.

THE VEDA OF THE SECOND WATERS

SACRAL CHAKRA ACTIVATION

The ancient mystics called this current Shakti, the dance of life's longing to know itself. Here it is rendered in verse: an offering for those learning to trust the ebb and flow of their own inner sea.

1. In the beginning was movement, and movement was holy.
The One became two so that it might feel its own reflection.
From that longing, the sacred waters were born and from the waters, the pulse of all creation.
2. Here the soul learns to taste its own existence.
The senses are the rivers of the divine and the body, a vessel for wonder.
To feel is not weakness; it is worship. For through pleasure, the Spirit remembers its joy.
3. Guard not against desire as an enemy but honor it as the fire beneath the wave. When it burns in balance, it births worlds.
When it floods in fear, it drowns them.
4.Thus, the wise one tends their inner sea, neither damming nor draining, yet as listening for the tide's true rhythm.
5. O seeker of sweetness, wash your grief and guilt in these living waters.
Let creation flow through you without shame.
For the moon within your belly is the same moon that commands the ocean's dance.
6. You are both the river and its source, the longing and its fulfillment.
Let your waters move and call it prayer.

SCRIPTURE OF THE INNER SUN

SOLAR PLEXUS ACTIVATION

For true power is the stillness of one who burns without consuming.

1.The fire within is the witness of all action.
It digests food and also experiences.
Through it, matter becomes meaning.
2. When the flame burns clear, the will is pure.
The self acts without trembling, and purpose aligns with the law of being.
3. When the flame burns wild, the self devours itself.
Pride rises, hunger multiplies and sight is lost in the smoke of wanting.
4. Power is not to conquer but to illuminate.
The true radiance warms others without burning them.
5. Discipline is devotion to the inner order.
Through restraint, the fire learns to serve.
6. The Goddesses said: Guard your fire well.
Feed it with truth, eliminate pride.
Let it warm, not scorch, illuminate, not blind.
7. In knowing this, the seeker becomes solar, a steady dawn in the midst
of chaos, lighting the path not by command, yet by being.
8. For when the fire in the belly bows to the light in the heart, you
become the dawn made human, gentle, bright, and sure of your own sky.

THE EMERALD FLAME

HEART CHAKRA ACTIVATION

The heart has never stood under fragility; it is the alchemist's crucible. Here, devotion shall not be bound to a deity but to life itself.

1. The heart is the bridge between earth and sky,
a green field where spirit takes human form and the human remembers spirit. Every pulse is a meeting of heaven and flesh.
2. Love is circulation, the rhythm by which life feeds itself.
To give is to breathe out; to receive is to breathe in.
Thus, the wise one learns to love as lungs do.
3. When grief comes, do not close.
The broken heart is not shattered glass but cracked earth, ready for rain.
Let tenderness be your teacher.
4. Pride hardens the chambers of compassion.
Humility restores their flow. The greatest power is to remain open
even in the presence of pain.
5. To forgive is to remember wholeness.
The heart does not erase, but divinely integrates.
Every wound becomes a window through which the light enters more freely.
6. Love never being anything to be found; love is revealed.
It was never outside you, only waiting
for your breath to slow enough to hear its song.
7. Beloved, guard not your heart like a fortress,
tend it like a garden. Let the world come to be nourished.
8. And when you love, let it be vast:
not for reward, nor for safety, but because your very being is
crafted from love.

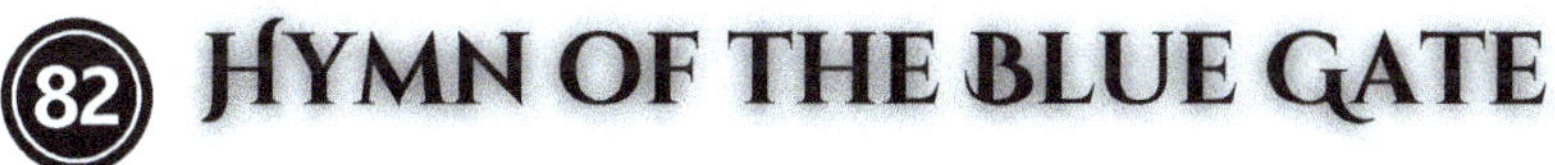

82 HYMN OF THE BLUE GATE

THROAT CHAKRA ACTIVATION

The ancients said the universe began with sound. If that is so, then every word we speak shapes creation anew.

1. Speech is the echo of thought;when the mind is pure, the voice becomes light.
2. A word born from anger cuts deeper than iron.
But a word shaped by calm heals without effort.
3. Restrain not the truth for fear of rejection;
silence born of fear breeds suffering.
4. Say only what is necessary, for excess speech clouds the spirit's mirror.
5. The wise speak as rivers flow,
with direction, with music, without haste.
6. To lie is to wound one's own tongue.
Let my speech be medicine, not weapon.
7. The one who speaks only after the heart has finished hearing, hears the power behind all words.
8. When the voice and the void walk side by side, all things sing in accord.
9. The throat is the sky's doorway within you, what passes through it shapes the weather of your life.
10. Blessed are the women who claim their voice, for they shall be known by the worlds they create through words spoken and sung.

INNER SKY

THIRD EYE ACTIVATION

In the still sky behind the brow,
the soul turns inward and meets its own vastness.

1. When the two eyes rest, the third awakens. The chase unto the light ceases, it becomes it.
2. Through this sight, time loosens its grip.
The soul remembers the pattern behind appearances, the silent geometry of destiny.
3. When vision is washed of desire, the whole cosmos is seen reflected in a single drop of being.
4. The eye that runs after illusion forgets its own eternal gaze.
Turn inward, there the infinite gazes back.
5. Those who cling to appearances drown in illusion.
Those who rest in awareness walk upon it like water.
6. The eye of flesh shows form, but the inner eye reveals essence.
One fades; the other is eternal.
7. Do not seek the future in omens, nor the past in memory.
The real is always now, waiting to be recognized.
8. The wise close their eyes to see more clearly, not to escape.
9. When perception and compassion unite,
the veil thins, and the heart becomes sight itself.

PROVERBS OF THE THOUSAND PETALS

CROWN CHAKRA ACTIVATION

The ancients called this awakening Sahasra, the lotus of infinite petals. When the lower roots are steady and the heart is open, this final blossom unfurls on its own, revealing that there was never a summit, only expansion without end.

1.The drop that knows the sea need not fear the tide.
When you remember your source, no wave can unmake you. All change becomes movement within the same vastness.

2. She who ceases to seek begins to see.
The eye that stops searching turns inward and discovers what was never lost.

3.The light above bows to the heart below.
Enlightenment is not ascent but union; the highest wisdom kneels before love.

4. When the mind kneels, heaven descends.
Only humility opens the crown. The proud stand tall beneath the gate and never pass through.

5. The wise never rise, they dissolve.
To ascend is to vanish as a separate self, merging with the radiance that birthed you. In surrender, all distance is erased.

6. The crown opens not upward, but inward.
True awakening is not escape from the body, but the realization that divinity already dwells within it.

7. The one who owns nothing possesses all.
Freedom begins when the hands unclench; emptiness is the lap in which abundance rests.

8. She who clings to light still stands in shadow.
Attachment, even to radiance, binds the seeker. True illumination requires release, not grasping.

9. The thousand petals bloom when the soul forgets its name.
When identity falls away, what remains is pure consciousness, vast, nameless, and at peace.

THE 99 NAMES OF SHE

Preface

This is a prayer, a poem, an act of remembering
A litany for every womxn who has ever been named, in love or in fear, in reverence or ridicule.
She has been called mother, goddess, whore, witch.
She has been crowned and crucified, exalted and erased.
She has carried names passed down by ancestors and muttered in back alleys. She has been worshiped in temples, judged in courts, and honored in kitchens and at bedsides.
The 99 Names of She are not meant to define her, they are meant to free her. To call in her fullness.
To gather her scattered faces and return them to her body.
To say: you are all of this, and more.

This is for the sacred and the profane, the polished and the raw, the divine and the defiant.
This is for the girl and the grandmother.
For the priestess and the baby mama.
For the enchantress and the activist.
For the one who tends altars and the one who burns them down.
This is a reflection, a spell, a love letter.
May these names remind us that She cannot be reduced.
She cannot be erased.
She IS.

THE 99 NAMES OF SHE

She is, Empress, Mother, Shakti, Goddess, Holy Spirit, Earth, Divine Feminine, Shekhinah, Pachamama, Sophia, Moon, Rose, Lotus, Venus, Matriarch, High Priestess, Midwife, Single Mother, Queen, Queen Mother, Wife, Ma, Abuela, Nana, Grandma, Yeye, Auntie, Daughter, Sis, Her, She, Lady, Madame, Miss, Miss Lady, Mrs., Señora, Bibi, Beloved, Love, Home Girl, MILF, Baby Mama.

She is Jezebel and Lilith, the original rebel; she is Feminist, Mistress, Courtesan, Seductress, Muse, Lover, Maiden, Crone, Oracle, Sibyl, Prophetess, Sensualist, Creatrix, Witch, Sorceress, Shamaness, Enchantress, Siren, Vixen, Wild womxn, Slut-Whore-Hoe, Baddie, Freak, Diva, Femme Fatale, Rebel, Outlaw, Angry Black womxn, Buffalo womxn, Serpent womxn, Black Widow, Damsel in Distress, Dyke, Bitch, Queer, Succubus, Stud, Housewife, Gold Digger.

Name HER Medicine womxn, Curandera, Herbalist, Warrior womxn, Huntress, Sis, Trap Queen, Ride or Die, Sky Dancer, Songstress, Fairy Godmother, Princess, Virgin, Eve, Spider Grandmother, weaver of worlds and stories.

She is Star womxn, the one who dances between galaxies and bones.
She is sacred and profane, tender and terrifying, instinctual and wise.
She is the nurturer and the destroyer, the sovereign and the servant, the lover, the visionary, the sensual, the shadow.
She is every name whispered in reverence or rebellion, the many faces of one eternal, untamable, holy force.
For she is a living sanctuary in every form.

For I am a living sanctuary in every form.
I AM Goddess. I AM Life.

THE FIRST HOME

THIS IS THE SONG OF THE BEGINNING.

1. I am the beginning before beginnings.
2. I am the threshold. The quiet, velvet universe that exists before the first breath.
3. I am woven into the very fabric of her, a deep, crimson chamber within the temple of her body. I feel the distant tides of her, the steady drum of her heart, the sigh of her lungs, the surge of her joy and the slow, heavy pull of her sorrow.
4. I am the most intimate part of her map, a place that exists only for a singular, sacred possibility.
5. I am the threshold. I am the memory of a universe, waiting once more in the quiet dark, having known the profound, temporary magic of creating a world.
6. I am architect and builder, nourisher and guardian. From the river of life that flows from her to me, I draw the raw materials, the water and the wine of existence and we begin to build a body.
7. I am the factory, the furnace, the fortress. I stretch and I expand, a universe obeying its own inevitable, expanding laws.
8. My sole purpose is to make space. To accommodate the miracle of form.
9. I am the dark where her unwritten novels find their first plot.
10. I am the silent, nurturing ground for the melody she cannot yet hum, the business she dreams of building, the art that haunts the corners of her mind. These are my ghost children. They have no heartbeat, yet they have a presence. They grow not as a body, but as a pressure, a luminous, demanding energy.
11. I am the first temple, the hidden throne, the altar of all things made flesh.
12. I am the moan that built worlds.
13. I am the blood that anointed them.
14. I am the Womb, unbroken, unending, forever creating, forever returning, forever whole.

PSALM OF THE WILLING VESSEL

1. Hear my prayer, Divine Source, Great Mother, Goddess,
Let the words of my mouth and the meditation of my heart
be acceptable in your sight, my rock and my redeemer.
2. Shape me as an instrument for your holy purpose.
Make me a flute for your melody of Divine works, a lantern for your unyielding light, a channel for your boundless love.
Selah.
3. Divine Feminine Force, use me, but for Your work, whatever it is, wherever it takes me, however it changes me.
Grant me hands that help, words that heal, and stillness that listens.
4. But I am but a vessel of flesh.
Therefore, fill me so that I may overflow.
Renew my spirit with the dew of your grace each dawn.
Feed my soul from the wellspring of your wisdom, that I may serve from abundance, nor from lack, nor from absence.
Selah.
5. Let every action be woven into your greater tapestry.
Let every connection serve the Highest Good for the healing of others, for the fulfillment of my path, for the gentle unfolding of your will in this world.
6. I make myself available as a willing channel for the Great Divine.
Through me may you speak, dance, sing and breathe.
Here I am. Use me. Guide me. Work through me.
May it be as you have ordained, from everlasting to everlasting.
7. Divine Source, I am yours.
Selah.

88 YES

1. I Am Life, and my native tongue is Yes.
2. I hereby decree that my existence is a conscious, willing, and glorious collaboration with the Universe. I align my will with the creative pulse of All That Is. From this moment forward, I choose arrival amidst avoidance, expansion amidst contraction, and the courageous yes of the heart over the fearful no of the mind.
3. I decree that I am fully present in this, my sacred temple.
4. I honor this body as the holy ground where Spirit meets Earth. I say Yes to its senses, its strength, its softness, and its wisdom. I move it with joy, nourish it with reverence, and rest it with gratitude. My body is not separate from my spirit; for it is the instrument through which my Yes becomes action. I inhabit it completely, without apology.
5. I decree that all parts of me are welcome and integrated.
6. I say a resounding Yes to my entirety, my light and my shadow, my joy and my grief, my power and my vulnerability. My scars are marks of survival, my tears are rivers of release, and my anger is a fire that forges my boundaries. I refuse to fragment myself. I reclaim every lost piece and make myself whole.
7. I decree that I am a conduit of divine creativity.
8. My voice, my hands, my mind, and my heart are instruments of creation. I will birth ideas, beauty, compassion, and change into this world. I allow the creative force to flow through me without obstruction. My very life is my masterpiece.
9. I decree that I am a nexus of sacred relationship.
10. I see the Divine in the eyes of my sisters and honor their journey as I honor my own. I say Yes to love that liberates, to community that upholds, and to connections that call me to my highest self. I offer my authentic presence and receive the gifts of others with an open heart. I am never alone.
11. My every breath is a Yes.
12. My every heartbeat is a Yes.
13. My every step is a Yes upon the path I am co-creating.
14. I am the author and the authority of my experience.

So it is decreed.
So it is manifest.

INDEX

THE MAGICKAL KEYS

Here, each key reveals how the prayers can be used across purposes:
to call in love, to draw abundance, to cleanse the spirit, to ignite sensual power, to heal the womb, to open the intuitive gates, to release old patterns, to strengthen ancestry, to enter the mystical, and to embody the feminine arts.

The Keys teach that a verse is never one thing.
A line written for protection may also open roads.
A womb prayer may also heal grief.
A prosperity verse may also restore confidence.

Every page in this book carries multiple frequencies and the Keys show you how to unlock them.

This section is a map:
a way to navigate the prayers by intention, timing, and desire.
Whether you seek tenderness or fire, clarity or change, purification or power, the Keys offer a path into practical, spiritual, and emotional magic.

Think of The Keys as your grimoire index, your spellbook companion, your guide for weaving the sacred into everyday life.
You will find:

- how to choose verses for specific intentions
- when to speak them (moon phases, days, emotional moments)
- how to use them in baths, candles, mirrors, oils, breathwork
- which prayers amplify each other
- how to turn ordinary acts, cooking, cleaning, dressing, bathing, into living spells

The Book of Keys is the bridge between the mystical and the mundane.

COMPLETE PROTECTION KEY

Verses & Workings for:
shielding, cleansing, banishing, justice, reversal, and uncrossing.

v5 (Decree of Protection — pg. 11): Speak over front + back doors to seal the house in an impenetrable shield. Good for new homes, hotels, or after moving.
v3-5 (The Throne Reclaimed — pg. 9): Use during transitions (new job, move, relationship shift) to sever old agreements and establish new footing. Claim leadership over life.
v10 (Curse Breaker — pg. 17): Chant over uncrossing baths, egg cleanses, or salt scrubs to snap lingering hexes + inherited malocchio patterns.
v9 (Road Shield — pg. 12): Repeat while touching your steering wheel, plane seat, or train window for safe travel and protection from accidents.
v5-6 (Reclaiming My power — pg. 13): Use before hard conversations, family gatherings, or work meetings to shield your energy + prevent emotional manipulation.
v4-7 (Evil Eye Remover — pg. 14): Speak while cleansing your aura with smoke, Florida water, or cologne to strip envy, jealousy, and silent resentment from your field.
v2-3 (Luck & Divine Favor — pg. 28): Whisper before interviews, auditions, or important emails for protection from sabotage and to call in favorable outcomes.
v5-8 (Sacred Courage — pg. 39): Speak while planning to leave abusive or unsafe situations; a courage shield for exits + escape plans.
v3-6 (The Golden Feminine — pg. 43): Anoint your pulse points and say these lines when entering rooms that once intimidated you, boardrooms, family tables, spiritual spaces.
v10-13 (Glamour Magick — pg. 44): Use while getting dressed or doing makeup to cloak yourself in charm that deflects envy and malice without dimming your shine.
v11 (Invocation for the Sacred Self — pg. 94): Use as a psychic firewall when past partners, friends, or communities try to pull you back into old versions of yourself.
v8 (Return to Sender Spell — pg. 145): Use when someone is actively working against your freedom, case, or reputation; sends malice, lies, and curses back without you carrying their karma.
v5-7 (Return to Sender Spell — pg. 145): Use when you suspect active malice, gossip, or spiritual attack; best over mirrors, black candles, and reversal work.
v3-5) (She Who Remembers Herself— pg. 148): Pray while working money + love uncrossing's to specifically cancel patterns of poverty + heartbreak.
v5-9 (The Unbinding Prayer — pg. 152): Use to dissolve binding spells, oaths, and control dynamics (including religious or familial) that limit your free will.
v7-10 (Pussy Prayer — pg. 54): Whisper over your womb + yoni after harm, shame, or boundary violations; protection of the erotic self as sacred ground.
v12-15 (Sex Worker Prayer — pg. 60): Speak before work to call in safe clients, clear intuition, and protection from violence, exploitation, and spiritual residue.
v2-8 (The Unbinding Prayer — pg. 152): Use for karmic or generational legal patterns—family always in court, always in debt, always under scrutiny. Break spiritual contracts that keep the cycle going.
v8-11 (The Sacred Womb — pg. 78): Say when pregnant or calling in pregnancy, asking for spiritual protection around mother, baby, and the birth portal.
v14-16 (A Yoni Blessing— pg. 80): Recite to protect your feminine essence from being drained by caretaking, ministry, or emotional labor.

COMPLETE PROSPERITY KEY

verses for:
wealth, quick cash, bills, career, opportunity, influence, and long-term abundance.

Core Wealth & Abundance

v2–4 (Code of Plenty — pg. 21): Speak over coins/cash for steady financial flow. Thursdays, waxing moon.
v6–7 (Code of Plenty — pg. 21): Whisper while paying bills for ease + circulating wealth. Mondays.
v9–10 (Code of Plenty — pg. 21): Burn verses on bay leaves for quick money + open doors. New moon.
v8–11 (Prosperous womxn — pg. 23): Anoint gold candle for feminine prosperity + opulence. Fridays.
v3–5 (Overflowing Cup — pg. 31): Recite over water to multiply financial blessings. Daily.
v7-9 (Money, Power, Respect — pg. 27): Write verses on checks/currency for raises + recognition. Workdays.
v9-10 (Luck & Divine Favor — pg. 29): Speak into coins for gambling, raffles, windfalls. Thursdays.
v2–3 (Sun in My Steps — pg. 41): Bless shoes to walk into fortune + promotions. Mondays.
v5 (Command of Creation — pg. 24): Whisper over job apps, resumes, or business plans to manifest work. Waxing moon.
v9-10 (Employment Prayer — pg. 33): Place verses under resumes for hiring luck. Wednesdays.

Prosperity, Financial Favor & Profit Verses (Non-Money Prayers)

v7-8 (Everywhere I Go, I Am Loved — pg. 86): Charisma brings promotions, allies, financial favor. Daily before work.
v5-7 (Glamour Magick — pg. 44): Social magnetism draws opportunities + networks. Before meetings.
v3-5 (Beautiful Soul — pg. 50): Confidence attracts clients and benefactors. Daily self-care.
v1-3 (Psalm for Justice — pg. 15): Fair wages + just contracts. Tuesdays.
v2 (Sacred Courage — pg. 39): Bravery to request raises or launch new ventures. New beginnings.
v7-9 (Golden Feminine — pg. 43): Radiance attracts wealth + influential patrons. Fridays.
v4-5 (Righteous Alliance — pg. 135): Ancestral blessing strengthens financial foundations. Saturdays.
v10 (Great Mother's Prayer — pg. 127): Abundant nurturing ensures resources flow to family. Sundays.
v16 (Healer's Prayer — pg. 131): Restored vitality increases work stamina + prosperity. Mornings.
v6 (Witch's Prayer — pg. 129): Passion ignites financial success. Midnight.
v1-2 (Creative Flame — pg. 123): Creativity becomes income or new ventures. New moon.
v4 (Scroll of the Inner Eye — pg. 125): Foresight for wise money decisions. Waxing moon.
v9 (Unending Oracle — pg. 121): Manifestation + spiritual attunement. Fridays.
v4 (A Returning Dawn — pg. 91): Financial recovery after loss or debt. Sunrise.
v2 (Grief Release Decree — pg. 139): Release scarcity mindset + emotional financial blocks. Waning moon.
v6 (Self-Forgiveness Prayer — pg. 114): Heal shame around money or past mistakes. Anytime.
v8-9 (Wholeness Scripture — pg. 103): Balance spending, saving, investing. Daily.
v2 (Curse Breaker — pg. 17): Uncross financial blockages. Waning moon.
v8-9 (Return to Sender — pg. 145): Reverse envy or malice blocking success. Wednesdays.
v1 (Decree of Protection — pg. 11): Guard wealth from theft, misuse, and spiritual drain. Daily threshold work.

Career, Work & Social Influence

v3-4 (Business Success Invocation — pg. 26): Speak over contracts for profitable partnerships. Mondays.
v3 (Awakened Heart— pg. 84): Sweeten employers/clients for smoother deals. Fridays.
v8 (Sun in My Steps — pg. 41): Guidance in career pathways + steady advancement. Mondays.
v8 (Unbound — pg. 105): Release toxic jobs/agreements to step into freedom. Saturn hour.
v8 (Command for the Return of Light — pg. 101): Illuminate hidden opportunities. Sunrise.
v8 (Honey for the Imposter — pg. 112): Shield from fraud, shady employers, and bad deals. Wednesdays.

LOVE KEY

Verses & Workings for:
love, relationship, family, friendship, and soulmate work.

Romantic Love & Soulmate Union
v3, v7, v12 (Call of True Love — pg. 87): Two pink candles tied together for soulmate bonds. Fridays, Venus hour.
v7 (A Returning Dawn — pg. 91): Burn lavender with verse to restore separated love. Sunrise.
v8 (The Great Covenant — pg. 96): Write on parchment place under mattress for fidelity + devotion. Full moon.
v5 (Invocation for the Sacred Self — pg. 94): Mirror recitation to anchor self-love before any love spell. Daily.
v9 (Unbound — pg. 105): Burn verses with old love tokens to release heartbreak. Waning moon.
Passion, Desire & Sensual Love
v3 (The Witch's Prayer — pg. 129): Red candle + cinnamon oil to ignite passion. Fridays
v11 (The Unending Oracle — pg. 121): Whisper while applying perfume for allure + magnetism. Daily.
v9 (Creative Flame — pg. 123): Speak before sex or art to merge erotic fire with creation. New moon.
v10 (Empress of Existence — pg. 161): Recite into jewelry to enhance irresistible presence. Fridays, Venus hour.
v9 (The Gospel of Pleasure— pg. 58): Light a pink or white candle and read the prayer as an act of self-devotion. Waxing moon.
Friendship, Social Circle & Harmony
v1 (Everywhere I Go, I Am Loved — pg. 86): Speak into water and sip for attraction and kindness. Morning.
v3 (Stewardship of the Temple — pg. 93): Anoint with oils for self-care-based social magnetism. Before gatherings.
v5 (The Entrepreneur's Prosperity Prayer — pg. 26): Recite over invites or resumes to draw supportive allies. Mondays.
v3 (The Golden Feminine — pg. 43): Speak before events to radiate magnetic presence. Fridays.
Family & Ancestral Love
v4-5 (Restoration of the Mother–Daughter Bond — pg. 116): Place two candles apart, speak the verse, then move them closer → energetic reconciliation ritual. SUNRISE
v8 (Prayer to Release Karmic Debt in the Family Line of Women — pg. 152): Burn with ancestral incense for lineage love healing. Saturdays.
v10 (The Great Mother's Prayer — pg. 127): Light white candle to call in maternal unity. Sundays.
v8 (The Healer's Prayer — pg. 131): Recite with rosemary smoke to bless family health + affection. Wednesdays.
Reconciliation & Forgiveness
v7 (Decree of Reconciliation — pg. 98): Burn written prayer with rose petals to restore peace in relationships. Fridays.
v9 (Self-Forgiveness Prayer — pg. 114): Mirror verse to soften guilt + reopen the heart. Anytime.
v11-13 (Grief Release Decree — pg. 139): Chant in lavender bath to release heartbreak. Waning moon.
v5 (A Liturgy for Letting Go — pg. 147): Burn verses with old letters/photos to clear toxic ties. Dark moon.
v3 (Cord Cutting Prayer — pg. 141): Recite during cord-cutting to sever lingering love attachments. Saturn hour.
Everyday Warmth & Attraction
v5-6 (Psalm of the Road — pg. 12): Recite before travel for safe new connections + chance encounters. Before journeys.
v6 (Everywhere I Go, I Am Loved — pg. 86): Daily charm whispered before leaving home. Morning routine.
v4 (Overflowing Cup — pg. 31): Speak over meals for joyful, loving household energy. Family dinners.
v6 (Beautiful Soul — pg. 50): Recite while dressing to radiate inner beauty + draw affection. Daily.

Healing Key

Verses & Workings for:
emotional, physical, spiritual, womb, ancestral, or energetic healing

Core Healing Prayers

v3 (The Awakened Heart — pg. 84): Pour water over head in shower to cleanse illness + sorrow. Sundays, sunrise.
v5–6 (Sovereignty— pg. 37): Recite before creative projects or dancing, healing the inner child
v4–5 (Prayer for Womb Healing — pg. 77): Whisper while placing both hands over your womb to soothe grief. Fridays.
v12 (Blessing for the Womb in Mourning — pg. 67): Place a white flower in water → offer love and remembrance to the spirit of the child. New moon.
v3-4 (The Unbinding Prayer — pg. 152): Hold clear quartz + chant to balance mind and body. Sundays.
v2–3 (Self-Forgiveness Prayer — pg. 114): Recite in mirror to heal guilt, shame, self-blame. Anytime.
v3–5 (Grief Release Decree — pg. 139): Chant in lavender + salt bath to soften heartbreak + depression. Waning moon.
v7-8 (Unbound — pg. 105): Recite during smoke cleansing to heal trauma cords. Saturn hour.
v10–11 (Restoration of the Mother–Daughter Bond — pg. 116): Pour blessed water into earth for generational healing. New moon.
v7–8 (A Divine Decree for Breakthrough — pg. 143): Open windows + chant to call healing light. Sunrise.

Trauma Healing Verses (Non-Healing Prayers)

v1 (The Great Mother's Prayer — pg. 127): Maternal healing for family wounds. Sundays.
v2 (Righteous Alliance — pg. 135): Ancestors restore harmony + inner strength. Saturdays.
v6 (Psalm for Justice — pg. 15): Heal after injustice + restore inner peace. Tuesdays.
v2 (A Journey Home — pg. 156): Heal self-doubt + reclaim feminine power. Fridays.
v7 (Beautiful Soul — pg. 50): Heal self-worth wounds via mirror magick. Morning ritual.
v6 (Sacred Courage — pg. 39): Heal fear + trauma, restore bravery. Waxing moon.
v11 (The Witch's Prayer — pg. 129): Erotic recovery + passion healing. Fridays at midnight.
v8-9 (The Unending Oracle — pg. 121): Heal inner conflict; reconcile sacred + profane. Fridays.
v3-4 (Creative Flame — pg. 123): Burn away creative blocks + emotional stagnation. New moon.
v1 (Scroll of the Inner Eye — pg. 125): Heal confusion + restore intuitive clarity. Waxing moon.
v6-7 (The Prosperous womxn — pg 23): Heal scarcity trauma + money wounds. Thursdays.
v9-10 (A Returning Dawn — pg. 91): Heal from heartbreak, betrayal, emotional collapse. Sunrise.
v4 (Sun in My Steps — pg. 41): Heal lethargy + depression with movement + light. Mondays.
v4–5 (Decree of Protection — pg. 11): Heal anxiety + fear through warm water ritual. Evening baths.
v3 (Curse Breaker — pg. 17): Heal generational wounds + uncross inherited illness. Waning moon.
v10 (Return to Sender — pg. 145): Heal insomnia + mental clutter by banishing intrusion. Nighttime.
v9 (Overflowing Cup — pg. 31): Heal family/community emotional bonds. Gatherings.
v2 (Everywhere I Go, I Am Loved — pg. 86): Heal loneliness + restore openness to love. Daily.
v9 (Invocation for the Sacred Self — pg. 94): Heal self-image → foundation of recovery. Morning mirror work.

Everyday Healing & Self-Care

v5 (Stewardship of the Temple — pg. 93): Use with body oils for daily self-healing + nourishment. After bathing.
v5-6 (Honey for the Imposter — pg. 112): Heal false identity + restore authentic self. Wednesdays.
v4 (A Liturgy for Letting Go — pg. 147): Burn old letters/photos to heal heartbreak + grief. Dark moon.
v9 (Command for the Return of Light — pg. 101): Heal depression + invoke clarity + joy. Sunrise.

SENSUAL KEY

Verses & Workings for:
desire, charm, beauty, magnetism, erotic healing, or sacred embodiment.

Core Sensual & Erotic Prayers

v8-9 (Pussy Prayer — pg. 54): Speak over red candle to awaken sacred sexuality + root energy. Fridays, waxing moon.
v7 (Sex Worker Prayer — pg. 60): Recite before adornment to attract respect + financial allure. Before shifts.
v10 (The Gospel of Pleasure— pg. 58): Whisper in rose bath to amplify seduction + erotic magnetism. Fridays, Venus hour.
v8–9 (Sensual Soul — pg. 56): Anoint body with honey + verses to embody sensual confidence. New moon baths.
v13 (Sacred Courage — pg. 39): Use verses in dance/touch to release shame + embody sensual bravery. Fridays.
v14-15 (Glamour Magick — pg.44): Trace verses on mirror with rosewater to enhance allure + mystique. Before dates.
v4 (Beautiful Soul — pg. 50): Speak while dressing to glow with sensual radiance. Daily mornings.

Hidden Sensual Verses (Non-Sensual Prayers)

v7 (The Witch's Prayer — pg. 129): Ignite erotic fire + kundalini through movement. Midnight rites.
v11-12 (The Unending Oracle — pg. 121): Stand before a mirror naked or partially uncovered, speak the verse → integrate erotic and spiritual identity. + Shame release. Fridays.
v3 (Creative Flame — pg. 123): Sexual energy fuels creativity + seduction. New moon.
v10 (The Golden Feminine — pg. 43): Radiance + sovereignty amplify sensual power. Fridays.
v11 (Invocation for the Sacred Self — pg. 94): Self-love foundation for sensual magnetism. Morning mirror rites.
v6-7 (The Great Mother's Prayer — pg. 127): Fierce passion + gentleness for erotic healing. Full moon.
v8-9 (Sun in My Steps — pg. 41): Steps infused with vitality draw attention + sensual presence. Mondays.
v6 (Overflowing Cup — pg. 31): Love verses cross-purposed for intimacy + affection.
v6 (Everywhere I Go, I Am Loved — pg. 86): Social warmth becoming soft erotic magnetism. Daily charm.
v6-8 (The Healer's Prayer — pg. 131): Transformative + erotic rebirth + confidence. Fridays.
v5 (Scroll of the Inner Eye — pg. 125): Soft glamour for mystique. Waxing moon.
v5 (Empress of Existence — pg. 161): Mirror spell → boost self-confidence + dissolve smallness. Venus hour.

Sensual Healing & Everyday Magnetism

v5 (Prayer for Womb Healing — pg. 77): Gentle sensual self-touch with verses to heal intimacy trauma. Fridays.
v12 (Wholeness Scripture — pg. 103): Shadow Offering Ritual: Speak while journaling to soften resistance and self-judgment. + pleasure. Sundays.
v2–4 (Self-Forgiveness Prayer — pg .114): Release guilt and shame around sexuality. Anytime.
v8 (Grief Release Decree — pg. 139): Sensual lavender + Rose bath to release heartbreak. Waning moon.
v12 (A Returning Dawn — pg. 91): Rekindle affection + desire after loss. Sunrise.
v6 (Decree of Sacred Reconciliation — pg. 98): Restore sensual harmony in strained relationships. Fridays.
v5 (Righteous alliance— pg. 135): Ancestors bless sensual safety + boundaries. Saturdays.
v13 (Return to Sender — pg. 145): Protect sensual energy from envy + gossip. Nighttime.

WOMB KEY

Verses & Workings for:
menstruation, fertility, pregnancy, abortion, miscarriage, menopause, lineage healing, sexual vitality, creative womb power,

Menstrual Cycle, Flow & Release

v1–2 (Invocation of the Red Flow — pg. 65): Recite over cinnamon tea → call timely arrival of period.
v1–2 (1st Blood Rites of Passage — pg. 71): Light hibiscus candle → bless initiation into womxnhood. First menstruation.
v12 (Blessing for the Womb in Mourning — pg. 67): Pour water into soil → release grief after miscarriage or abortion. Dark moon.
v1–2 (The Womb's Rest — pg. 69): Speak verses when resting → restore womb after abortion or heavy cycle. Saturdays.
v2 (A Liturgy for Letting Go — pg. 147): Burn with dried rose petals → release stagnant cycle energy. Waning moon.
v7 (Grief Release Decree — pg. 139): Lavender bath + verses → heal womb sorrow. Tuesdays

Fertility, Pregnancy & Creative Womb Power

v6-7 (Prayer for Womb Healing — pg. 77): Anoint belly with rosewater → heal + bless fertility.
v8 (The Sacred Womb — pg.78): Speak verses over pomegranate seeds → healthy conception + gestation. Waxing moon.
v6–7 (Yoni Blessing — pg. 80): Whisper verses into bath → awaken sensual, fertile energy.
v2–4 (The Healers Prayer — pg. 131): Fire of transformation → strengthen reproductive vitality. Sundays.
v6 (Creative Flame — pg. 123): Direct sexual/womb energy into art, ritual, or business. Sunday
v11 (Wholeness Scripture — pg. 103): Light one candle for Girl, one for womxn, one for Fury, one for Tenderness. Chant the verse to unify them. Sundays.

Pregnancy Loss, Child Spirit & Lineage Healing

v5–6 (Song for the Child Who Dances in Heaven — pg. 75): Candle ritual → honor spirit of lost child. Anytime
v10 (Prayer for Child I Cannot Hold — pg. 154): Speak with white rose → healing after miscarriage or stillbirth. Waning moon.
v2-3 (The Unbinding Prayer — pg. 152): Free ancestral trauma around womb + birth.Saturdays.
v6 (Restoration of the Mother–Daughter Bond — pg.116): Recite over a bowl of water, then wash hands/face → restores emotional clarity. → mend womb-line between mothers + daughters. Sunrise.
v7 (The Great Mothers Prayer — pg. 127): Sit on the ground or floor while reciting → grounding, root chakra, stability, womb activation. Sundays. New moon or grounding work.

Menopause, Aging & Transition

v7-8 (Psalm of the Queen's Crown — pg. 73): Gold candle ritual → crown menopause as wisdom + power. Full moon
v5-8 (The Prosperous womxn — pg. 23): Speak verses with anointing oil → abundance + vitality in new phase. Anoint hands & feet. Fridays.
v11 (The Golden Feminine — pg .43): Strengthen radiance during life transitions. Fridays.
v7 (Sun in My Steps — pg. 41): Walk in morning sun → restore energy post-menopause. Daily.

Hidden Womb Verses (Non-Womb Prayers)

v5 (Invocation for the Sacred sself — pg. 94): Self-love verse → strengthens womb as creative center. Morning mirror rites.
v2 (Sacred Courage — pg. 39): Reclaim womb power after trauma. Waxing moon.
v5–7 (The Unending Oracle of the Divine Self — pg. 121): Integrate heart+ sexual + womb identities. anytime
v2–3 (Waters of Forgiveness — pg. 114): Release womb shame + guilt. Anytime.
v6 (Curse Breaker — pg. 17): Uncross generational womb trauma. Waning moon.
v14 (Return to Sender Spell — pg. 145): Deflect jealousy/envy tied to fertility or womxnhood. Night work.
v9 (The Overflowing Cup — pg. 31): Bless womb as source of creative overflow. Shared meals.
v1-2 (Beautiful Soul — pg. 50): Heal body image, affirm womb beauty. Daily self-care.
v5 (Prayer for Justice — pg. 15): Demand fair treatment of womb, body, rights. Tuesdays.
v2 (Command for the Return of Light — pg. 101): Shine light into hidden womb places → healing. Sunrise.

WOMXNLY ARTS KEY

Verses & Workings for:
radiance, cycles, glamour, sensuality, magnetism, fertility, authority, beauty, and creative power.

Beauty, Glamour & Radiance

v2 (Glamour Magick — pg. 44): Trace verses on mirror with rosewater → enhance allure. Before social outings.
v3 (Beautiful Soul — pg. 50): Speak while dressing → glow with confidence + radiance. Daily.
v3-4 (Empress of Existence — pg. 161): Recite into jewelry → irresistible beauty, power + command. Fridays.
v1-2 (The Golden Feminine — pg. 43): Sunrise ritual → sovereignty, regal beauty. Fridays.
v10 (Scroll of the Inner Eye — pg. 125): Intuitive downloads → Empowerment before divination or readings. anytime

Sensuality, Magnetism & Erotic Power

v2–3 (Pussy Prayer — pg. 54): Red candle → awaken sacred sexuality. Fridays, waxing moon.
v8–9 (Sensual Soul — pg. 56): Lip Honey anointing → sensual confidence. New moon.
v5–6 (Sex Worker Prayer — pg. 60): Verses during adornment → erotic dignity + financial magnetism. Before work.
v3–5 (The Witches Prayer — pg. 129): Serpent fire → erotic charge + vitality. Midnight rituals.
v3 (The Unending Oracle of the Divine Self — pg. 121): Whore/holy. Light/shadow integration → magnetic paradoxical allure. Fridays.
v10 (Creative Flame — pg. 123): Transform sensual energy into creativity + charm. New moon.

Womb Mysteries & Feminine Cycles

v1–2 (Invocation of the Red Flow — pg. 65): Cinnamon tea → timely menstruation. New moon.
v1–4 (1st Blood Rites of Passage — pg. 71): Hibiscus candle → bless maidenhood. First menstruation. Inner girl acknowledgment for womxn.
v4–6 (Blessing for the Womb in Mourning — pg .67): Speak outdoors with bare feet on the earth to return grief to the soil for gentle transmutation. Dark moon.
v9-10 (Prayer for Womb Healing — pg.77): Rosewater anointing → heal womb + heart. Fridays.
v3-5 (Yoni Blessing — pg. 80): Place a hand over your yoni and recite → Feminine power activation + sensual sovereignty. Fridays. New moon
v5–6 (Blessing of Pregnancy — pg. 78): Speak with pomegranate → healthy pregnancy.
v1 (Psalm of the Queen's Crown — pg. 73): Gold candle →Speak at sunrise to claim power in transition. Full moon.

Confidence, Power & Inner Authority

v9–10 (She Who Stands — pg.46): Barefoot on earth → rooted feminine power. Saturn day.
v4 (Scripture of the Shadow Feminine — pg. 48): Say at the lighting of a red candle to honor your shadow as a blessing. Daily.
v1-4 (The Prosperous womxn — pg. 23): Gold candle → wealth + power up femininity.
v1 (Spiritualist Psalm for Justice — pg. 15): Speak verses → demand dignity + respect for the feminine. Tuesdays.
v3 (Celebrating Womxnhood — pg. 51): Place a flower or fruit on your altar → honor your current life stage + feminine rebirth. Full moon. Birthdays, seasonal changes, moon phases.
v5 (The Great Mothers Prayer — pg. 127): Anoint your forehead with oil while reciting → activate intuition, psychic senses, creative flow. Waxing moon or before divination.

Hidden womxnly Arts Verses (Non-Feminine-Specific Prayers)

v5 (Everywhere I Go, I Am Loved — pg. 86): Magnetism that amplifies social + feminine charm.
v15-16 (The Overflowing Cup — pg. 31): Gratitude ritual → embody feminine abundance + generosity. Shared meals.
v10 (Curse Breaker — pg. 17): Uncross womb/feminine lineages → reclaim sovereignty.
v4 (Return to Sender Spell — pg. 145): Deflect envy against beauty, sensuality, or feminine power. Evenings
v9-10 (Wholeness Scripture — pg. 103): Dance slowly to reconnect fractured parts of self.
v7 (A Returning Dawn — pg. 91): Renewal → fresh feminine beginnings. Sunrise.
v9 (Command for the Return of Light — pg. 101): Radiance restored → feminine glow reawakened. At dawn.

RELEASE KEY

Verses & Workings for:
release, banishing, surrender, endings, and emotional unclenching.

Core Release & Letting Go Prayers
v5–6 (A Liturgy for Letting Go — pg. 147): Burn with old letters or photos → release attachments + stale emotions. Dark moon.
v1–2 (Cord Cutting Prayer — pg. 141): Cut string while chanting verses → sever toxic ties. Saturn hour.
v2 (Unbound — pg. 105): Speak during smoke cleansing → release binding contracts + trauma cords. Waning moon.
v3–4 (Grief Release Decree — pg. 139): Lavender bath → release sorrow + heartbreak. Waning moon.
v5 (Waters of Forgiveness / Self-Forgiveness Prayer — pg. 114): Whisper into mirror → release guilt + self-blame. Anytime.
v10 (Curse Breaker — pg. 17): Burn Bay leaf + black candle → release hexes + energy blockages. Waning moon.
v12-13 (Return to Sender Spell — pg. 145): Recite when sensing malice → release intrusion from others. Night work.
Hidden Release Verses (Non-Release Prayers)
v7 (Sacred Courage — pg. 39): Release fear + reclaim strength. Waxing moon.
v7 (Beautiful Soul — pg. 50): Release insecurity, step into self-love. Daily self-care.
v5-6 (The Golden Feminine — pg. 43): Release silencing of the feminine voice. Fridays.
v2-3 (Decree of Protection — pg. 11): Release anxiety into a river → calm nervous system. Evening baths.
v9-10 (**Sun in My Steps — pg. 41):** Release lethargy → walk into renewed energy. Mondays.
v3 (Everywhere I Go, I Am Loved — pg. 86): Release loneliness + invite warmth. Daily charms.
v7-8 (A Returning Dawn — pg. 91): Release grief from endings, welcome renewal. Sunrise.
v6 (The Great Mothers Prayer — pg. 127): Release anger into Mother's embrace. Sundays.
v1 (Righteous Alliance — pg. 135): Release burdens into ancestral hands. Saturdays.
v1 (Wholeness Scripture — pg 103): Deepens intuition, reduces self-rejection, strengthens psychic clarity. Sundays.
v2 (Creative Flame — pg. 123): Release blocks to creativity + self-expression. New moon.
v4-5 (**The Healers Prayer — pg. 131):** Release stagnation → ignite renewal. Anytime.
v7-8 (Scroll of the Inner Eye — pg. 125): Release distraction → sharpen focus. Waxing moon.
v1-3 (Command for the Return of Light — pg. 101): Release heaviness into flame → restore clarity. Dawn.
Release in Womb & Lineage Work
v4–6 (Blessing for the Womb in Mourning — pg. 67): Inhale lavender or chamomile steam → call peace into the body.
v3 (The Womb's Rest — pg. 69): Release exhaustion, restore womb strength. Saturdays.
v9 (The Unbinding Prayer — pg. 152): Release generational pain from the female line. Saturdays.
v1–5 (Restoration of the Mother–Daughter Bond — pg. 116): Burn the verse with rose petals → release verbal wounds and emotional triggers. Waning moon.
v5 (Psalm of the Queen's Crown — pg. 73): Release youth, recite while brushing skin with salt/sugar scrub → symbolic shedding. Full moon.
v7 (Prayer for Child I Cannot Hold — pg. 154): Release spirit of unborn/lost child with grace. Waning moon.
v5-6 (Song for the Child Who Dances in Heaven — pg. 75): Release grief while honoring child's spirit. Full moon.
Everyday Release Uses
v6 (Spiritualist Psalm for Justice — pg. 15): Release resentment after unfairness. Tuesdays.
v3 (Honey for the Imposter — pg. 112): Release false voices + impostor syndrome. Wednesdays.
v5 (**Invocation for the Sacred Self — pg. 94):** Release self-criticism in mirror rituals. Morning routine.
v3 (The Overflowing Cup — pg. 31): Release fear of scarcity → embody abundance.
v4 (Spiritualist Psalm for Justice — pg. 15): Release money anxiety, call in flow. Thursdays.

ANCESTRAL KEY

Verses & Workings for:
ancestor veneration, lineage healing, generational protection, and receiving ancestral blessings.

Core Lineage & Ancestral Prayers

v9 (Prayer to Release Karmic Debt of Women — pg. 152): Burn verses with ancestral incense → release generational pain. Saturdays, waning moon.
v1 (Restoration of the Mother-Daughter Bond — pg. 116): Pour water into soil for libation → invites ancestral feminine presence to mediate, soften, and protect the relationship. New moon.
v5-6 (Song for the Child Who Dances in Heaven — pg. 75): Light candle → honor children in the ancestral realm. Full moon.
v4-5 (Prayer for Child I Cannot Hold — pg. 154): White rose offering → release grief into ancestor care. Waning moon.
v5 (Psalm of the Queen's Crown — pg. 73): Use at thresholds (doors, gates, intersections) to call wisdom from the beyond. Full moon.
v1 (The Great Mother's Prayer — pg. 127): Light a candle and bow your head → receive maternal ancestral embrace. Sundays, family gatherings, womb rituals.
v5-7 (Righteous Alliance — pg.135): Ancestral armor → protection, guidance, justice. Saturdays.

Hidden Ancestral Verses (Non-Ancestral Prayers)

v2-3 (Decree of Protection — pg. 11): Speak at thresholds → ancestors guarding the home. Night.
v2-3 (Spiritualist Psalm for Justice — pg. 15): Call ancestors to aid in fairness + defense. Tuesdays.
v7 (The Golden Feminine — pg. 43): Ancestors restore silenced feminine voices. Fridays.
v13 (Sacred Courage — pg. 39): Ancestors lend bravery in battle + hardship. Waxing moon.
v13-15 (The Healers Prayer — pg. 131): Ancestors as healers → call them into body restoration. Anytime.
v1-2 (Creative Flame — pg. 123): Ancestors as muses → channel lineage creativity. New moon.
v5 (Scroll of the Inner Eye — pg. 125): Receive ancestral visions in dreams + meditation. Waxing moon.
v2 (Invocation for the Sacred Self — pg. 94): Anchor in self → embody ancestral strength. Morning ritual.
v14 (The Overflowing Cup — pg. 31): Meals as offerings → share verses at table for ancestors. Family feasts.
v8 (Sun in My Steps — pg. 41): Walk with ancestors' guidance → safe passage in life. Mondays.
v12-15 (Return to Sender Spell — pg. 145): Ancestors deflect envy + curses. Nighttime banishing.
v15-17 (Curse Breaker — pg. 17): Ancestors aid in uncrossing generational hexes. Waning moon.
v6-7 (Wholeness Scripture — pg. 103): expands presence to "make room" for ancestor contact. Sundays.
v7 (Everywhere I Go, I Am Loved — pg. 86): attract allies + protect socially. Daily charm.
v4 (A Returning Dawn — pg. 91): Ancestors guide reconciliation + new beginnings. Sunrise.

Ancestral Blessings & Offerings

v4-6 (The Prosperous womxn — pg. 23): Wealth blessings flowing through the matrilineal line. Fridays.
v1-2 (The Unending Oracle of the Divine Self — pg. 121): Beat a drum, stomp, or clap while reciting → release rage + Ancestral rites. Mars hour, Tuesdays.
v7 (The Witches Prayer — pg. 129): Ancestors awaken through serpent fire + bloodline power. Midnight rites.
v3 (Empress of Existence — pg. 161): Light purple candle → call divine placement + destiny alignment. sundays.
v1 (Celebrating Womxnhood — pg. 51): Light a gold or white candle and speak the verse → honor female ancestors. Sundays or during women's circles.
v9 (The Great Mothers Prayer — pg. 127): Balance fierce and gentle ancestral blessings. Sundays.

CORE BREAKTHROUGH & TRANSFORMATION KEY

Verses & Workings for:
change, renewal, success, and rebirth.

<u>**Core Breakthrough & Transformation Prayers**</u>
v7–8 (A Divine Decree for Breakthrough — pg. 143): Open windows at sunrise → invoke new paths + breakthroughs. Sunrise rituals.
v4–7 (Unbound — pg. 105): Smoke cleanse with verses → break chains + binding agreements. Waning moon.
v5–6 (A Liturgy for Letting Go — pg. 147): Burn verses with paper of obstacles → release blockages. Dark moon.
v4 (Scripture of the Shadow Feminine — pg. 48): Chant over candle → shadow work + transformations. New moon.
v13 (Sacred Courage — pg. 39): Call bravery to push through transformation. Waxing moon.
<u>**Hidden Breakthrough Verses (Non-Breakthrough Prayers)**</u>
v3 (A Returning Dawn — pg. 91): Speak at first light → fresh start, new chapter. Sunrise.
v6 (Decree of Reconciliation — pg. 98): Restore relationships → breakthrough in love or work. Fridays.
v9-11 (The Prosperous Womxn — pg. 23): Verses in gold candle → financial leveling-up. Thursdays.
v7 (Spiritualist Psalm for Justice — pg. 15): Triumph in courts or disputes → breakthrough into fairness. Tuesdays.
v8 (The Great Mothers Prayer — pg. 127): acceptance, surrender, grief integration, endings. Sunset
v4 (The Golden Feminine — pg. 43): Transformation into radiance + confidence. Fridays.
v15 (The Overflowing Cup — pg. 31): Verses over meals → overflow into expansion + growth. Shared meals.
v1–2 (Everywhere I Go, I Am Loved — pg. 86): Transform isolation into connection. Daily charm for making new connections.
v4 (Wholeness Scripture — pg. 103): Integrates shadow, reduces self-sabotage, restores emotional stability. Sundays.
v16 (The Healers Prayer — pg. 131): Transform pain into power. Anytime.
v3 (Return to Sender Spell — pg. 145): Breakthrough in peace by releasing gossip + harm. Night work.
v6-7 (Invocation for the Sacred Self — pg. 94): Self-anchoring verse → transformation through self-recognition. Morning mirror ritual.
<u>**Spiritual Ascension & Renewal**</u>
v6 (The Unending Oracle of the Divine Self — pg. 121): Invoke matriarchal wisdom → transformation through higher vision. Fridays.
v11–13 (Scroll of the Inner Eye — pg. 125): Chant before meditation → breakthrough in clarity + foresight. Waxing moon.
v10–11 (Sun in My Steps — pg. 41): Walk into breakthrough opportunities with verses. Mondays.
v7-8 (Prayer for Child I Cannot Hold — pg. 154): Transform grief into legacy + love. Waning moon.
v2 (Righteous Alliance — pg. 135): Ancestors clear path for destiny breakthroughs. Saturdays.
v2 (Empress of Existence — pg. 161): Stand barefoot, hand over heart → claim personal authority + self-worth. sunrise.
v2 (Celebrating Womxnhood — pg. 51): Recite while journaling → awakens matriarchal creative inspiration, storytelling magic, and spiritual voice. Sunrise or new moon.
v3 (Command for the Return of Light — pg. 101): protection → breakthrough after darkness. Sunrise.
v11-13 (Honey for the Imposter — pg. 112): activating confidence by releasing false masks. Wednesdays.

MYSTICAL KEY

verses for:
dreams, visions, divination, prophecy, intuition, spiritual sight, and hidden wisdom

Vision & Prophecy
v14 (The Healing Path — pg. 162): Place under pillow → dream prophecy, sharpen intuition. Waxing moon.
v9 (The Unending Oracle of the Divine Self — pg. 121): Speak the verse before meditation or divination → Opening psychic channels. dawn. new moon
v5 (The Witches Prayer — pg. 129): Chant at crossroads → awaken serpent sight, kundalini visions. Midnight rites.
v5 (Creative Flame — pg. 123): Light candle → channel creative downloads from spirit. New moon.
v7 (Command for Return of Light — pg. 101): inner Fire invocation → banish confusion, bring clarity of vision. Sunrise.
Divination & Spirit Sight
v10 (Invocation for the Sacred Self — pg. 94): Speak before tarot or scrying → center in truth. Before readings.
v2 (Righteous Alliance — pg. 135): Call ancestors into divination for truth + protection. Saturdays.
v3 (Spiritualist Psalm for Justice — pg. 15): Reveal hidden truth in disputes via divination. Tuesdays.
v6 (Wholeness Scripture — pg. 103): Balance energy before or after spiritual readings. Sundays.
v1 (Empress of Existence — pg. 161): Use verses with mirror scrying → allure + prophetic glamour. Fridays.
Dreams & Nocturnal Work
v10 (Sun in My Steps — pg. 41): Whisper before bed → seeding prosperity in dreams. Mondays.
v12 (The Healers Prayer — pg. 131): Speak at night → summon dream healers + visions. Nighttime.
v1 (Everywhere I Go, I Am Loved — pg. 86): Bedtime anointing + ancestral favor. Fridays.
v6 (The Great Mothers Prayer — pg. 127): Dream verses for maternal guidance + comfort. Sundays.
v4–5 (Decree of Protection — pg. 11): Whisper over pillow → guard from nightmares + psychic intrusion. Bedtime.
Spirit Contact & Mediumship
v3–4 (Righteous Alliance — pg. 135): Call ancestors into circle for messages. Saturdays.
v7-8 (Song for the Child Who Dances in Heaven — pg. 75): Light candle → receive dream messages from children in spirit. Full moon.
v11 (The Sacred Womb — pg. 78): Invoke spirit guides who specialize in mothering and caring for children in the unseen realm. Full moon.
v2-5 (Blessing of Pregnancy — pg. 78): Call on unborn or future spirits to commune. Waxing moon.
v6 (Curse Breaker — pg. 17): Break interference blocking spirit contact. Waning moon.
Mystical Verses (Non-Mystical Prayers)
v12 (A Returning Dawn — pg. 91): Sunrise verses → prophetic beginnings, omens of change. Sunrise.
v9 (The Overflowing Cup — pg. 31): Use at feasts → prophecy through communal intuition. Shared meals.
v3 (Return to Sender Spell — pg. 145): Scry smoke → reveal source of harm. Night banishing.
v1–2 (Sacred Courage — pg. 39): Verse in trance work → face shadow visions with strength. Waxing moon.
v6 (The Golden Feminine — pg. 43): Glamour + sovereignty sharpen intuitive reception. Fridays.
v3 (Celebrating Womxnhood — pg. 51): Recite at your altar with an open window → invite success, visibility, and spiritual purpose. Anytime you begin a new project or mission.
v7-8 (Honey for the Imposter — pg. 112): Reveal false spirits or deceptive energies. Wednesdays.

About The Author

> " What was erased in scripture survived in women. I listen there. "

Priestess St. Journey

High Priestess St. Journey is a Psychic Medium, Spiritualist, and Feminine Mystic who believes prayer should meet real life. Her work stands at the crossroads of foremother wisdom and embodied spirituality, where prayer becomes active declaration and conscious participation with the living Divine.

For over a decade, she has guided women and womxn back to their own sacred authority through readings, ritual, and the radical act of feeling pleasure without apology. Her own path was carved through grief, ceremonial practices, and the slow unlearning of inherited shame. What emerged was a voice that refuses to separate the holy from the human.

Book of Womxn: 88 Spiritual Prayers, Decrees & Rituals for the Divine Feminine is her first full collection. It is the fruit of years of listening, bleeding, receiving, and purging outdated narratives around womanhood.

St. Journey is based in Atlanta, where she tends her altar, her ancestors, and her own unclenched joy. She offers private sessions and virtual ceremonies. To walk with her, visit her website or find her on social media.

Contact Details:

www.sumgoodjuju.com
sumgoodjuju@gmail.com

www.ingramcontent.com/pod-product-compliance
Lightning Source LLC
LaVergne TN
LVHW050534100826
845148LV00002B/551